THE COACH'S COMPANION

WINNING
BASEBALL

FOR BEGINNER TO INTERMEDIATE PLAY

THE COACH'S COMPANION

WINNING BASEBALL

FOR BEGINNER TO INTERMEDIATE PLAY

Trent Mongero

STERLING

New York / London
www.sterlingpublishing.com

10 9 8 7 6 5 4 3 2 1

Produced by LightSpeed Publishing, Inc. and X-Height Studio

Published by Sterling Publishing Co., Inc.
387 Park Avenue South, New York, NY 10016
© 2011 by Trent Mongero
Distributed in Canada by Sterling Publishing
c/o Canadian Manda Group, 165 Dufferin Street
Toronto, Ontario, Canada M6K 3H6
Distributed in the United Kingdom by GMC Distribution Services
Castle Place, 166 High Street, Lewes, East Sussex, England BN7 1XU
Distributed in Australia by Capricorn Link (Australia) Pty. Ltd.
P.O. Box 704, Windsor, NSW 2756, Australia

Printed in China

Sterling ISBN 978-1-4027-5808-9

For information about custom editions, special sales, premium and corporate purchases, please contact Sterling Special Sales Department at 800-805-5489 or specialsales@sterlingpublishing.com.

DEDICATION

I would like to dedicate this book to my current and former baseball players. My memories of most of the wins and losses have faded over the years. What I do clearly recall are the times I spent with passionate young players who have now grown up to become productive citizens in our society—people of integrity! They are husbands, fathers, bankers, teachers, coaches, lawyers, salespeople, preachers, doctors, etc. There are also some who are still actively pursuing their dreams of playing in the Major Leagues. I hope they each can say that they learned much more than just baseball from our time together. Thanks for the wonderful memories.

In addition, I would like to dedicate this series of baseball books to FCA—Fellowship of Christian Athletes. FCA has made a big impact on my life and is currently making a significant, positive impact on the lives of coaches, athletes, and families of athletes around our county. By building a solid foundation in God, FCA is giving young people the character tools they need to lead lives of integrity.

FCA also places a heavy emphasis on nurturing coaches' families and developing their leadership skills. They recognize that it is very easy for dedicated coaches to lose perspective in their quest for winning and for their families to suffer as a result. My family will always treasure the first of what we hope will be many family vacations to St. Simons Island, Georgia, for the annual FCA Coaches' Family Camp. Please visit FCA's Web site (www.fca.org) to learn more about all the wonderful things FCA is doing to help coaches, their families, and athletes across our country.

Table of Contents

PART TWO

Outside the Lines 119

FOREWORD

THE GAME of baseball has been "Our National Pastime" for many generations and has now grown to a sport enjoyed across the globe. Most kids begin their journey in baseball dreaming of one day becoming a Major League player. They emulate their favorite stars in backyards, on the playground, and on their local ball diamonds. They close their eyes and imagine getting the game-winning hit or throwing a no-hitter to clinch the seventh game of the World Series. I, too, grew up with a goal of making it to the Major Leagues and I was fortunate to have several coaches along the way who taught me the finer points of the game and inspired me to reach my goal.

Many boys and girls grow up with the ability to be fundamentally sound baseball players, either as pitchers, hitters, defenders, catchers, or even base-stealers. Players are taught by their coaches and parents that practice makes perfect. Thus, they work day and night to improve their skills in order to become the best players possible. However, they find that practice doesn't make perfect. What is needed to reach their personal best is a combination of motivation, determination, correct instruction, positive reinforcement, practice, and persistence. Most of all, never give up in what you believe!

To assist coaches, players, and parents to reach their full potential, Trent Mongero, who is a former youth, high school, college, and professional player himself, has spent years away from his family in order to author and complete this educational series of baseball books and accompanying instructional DVDs. His deep knowledge, unmatched energy, and passion to help others, makes *The Coach's Companion* series of books a must read.

Through this detailed series of books and DVDs, you will be exposed to age-appropriate fundamental instruction and drills to correctly learn how to be a better coach, help your child improve, and play this great game with focus and precision. It will expose you to all facets of baseball including offensive and defensive skills, the mental side of the game, coaching insight, and what to expect if you are a college or a Major League prospect.

Even though I played Major League baseball, I will never stop learning about this great game. I wish *The Coach's Companion* series of books had been out twenty years ago because it would have only made me a better player. I hope you take the time to read this book and help make your baseball experiences rewarding. Now is the time for you to be the baseball coach, player, or parent you dream of being!

Trot Nixon
#7 Boston Red Sox
2004 World Series Champions

ACKNOWLEDGMENTS

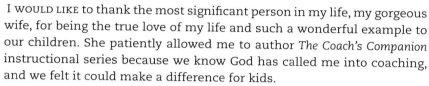

I WOULD LIKE to thank the most significant person in my life, my gorgeous wife, for being the true love of my life and such a wonderful example to our children. She patiently allowed me to author *The Coach's Companion* instructional series because we know God has called me into coaching, and we felt it could make a difference for kids.

I want to thank my son, Taber, and my daughter, Maris, who had to make the sacrifice of dealing with Daddy at the computer editing video and typing hours and hours on end. This three-book series has taken over four years from its innocent conception in Richmond County, North Carolina, to its completion in Gainesville, Georgia. It was written and rewritten three distinct times while balancing teaching, coaching, and spending valuable time with my family.

I would like to especially recognize The University of North Carolina at Wilmington along with North Hall High School and Gary Brown for granting me access to their fine baseball facilities to shoot the instructional video and still photos. I want to thank former big league player and current professional scout Tim Hyers and professional pitching coach Scott "Emo" Emerson for their contributions to the project.

Thanks to: J Wink (www.j-dub.biz) for providing the ball caps used in most of the project; Jim Haynes Photography for allowing me to use his action photos throughout the three books and accompanying DVDs; Beau DeHass for creating the song used in the DVD introduction; Davie Waggett, Kenneth Robinette, Rick Catlin, Jay Denham, Hal Shuler, and Richmond Senior High School for their various contributions to the original manual that eventually became the manuscript for this series of baseball instructional books.

Lastly, none of this would have been possible without the players and their families who spent many hours being filmed or photographed so they could help others enjoy the game of baseball.

INTRODUCTION

CONGRATULATIONS ON your purchase of *The Coach's Companion: Winning Baseball for Beginner to Intermediate Play*. This in-depth resource will provide coaches, parents, and players with a wealth of vital information to be successful in the game of baseball. This book contains the tools and resources you need to successfully teach and play the game, and to become a winner at every level of amateur baseball.

HOW TO GET THE MOST FROM THIS RESOURCE

Using 21st-century technology, *The Coach's Companion* offers the most comprehensive way to learn and teach a skill correctly. It utilizes the learning sequence of read, watch, comprehend, apply, evaluate, adjust, and reevaluate. This is not nearly as complicated as it sounds.

The earlier you are introduced to the basic concepts and skills in this book, the better you will become at coaching or playing baseball. This will create a solid foundation of knowledge that you can build upon for years to come. It is a literal building process; basic baseball skills and concepts are introduced and then added to at the appropriate time as the game progresses in speed and complexity. In other words, this book grows with you! If you are just starting to coach or play, this book is designed for you to enter and begin learning at your current level.

Time, or the lack of time, can rob us from being one-hundred percent effective as coaches or parents as we try to teach our children the game of baseball. If you are like the millions who love to coach but don't have time to read, *The Coach's Companion* is your answer. Because the book and the accompanying DVD are divided into small parts, you can review specific sections or watch segments of the DVD for practice, games, meetings, or on an as-needed basis. For the coach who can make time to read all three books and watch all accompanying DVDs in the series, this resource will provide hours of information that will help you comprehend the game of baseball as you never have before. Therefore, this entire instructional series is a "must have" in your baseball library.

The Coach's Companion is a life-long resource. It is my hope that you never outgrow this series of books as long as you love the game of baseball.

THE CHALLENGES OF COACHING AND PARENTING BASEBALL PLAYERS

Coaches face many issues and concerns, which they must effectively address if they are to inspire their teams and enjoy their coaching experiences. Well-versed coaches should know how to teach the fundamental skills, drills, and game situations, possess effective strategies to deal with parents, be able to manage their players and staff, know how to organize a practice, and be capable of organizing effective fundraisers for their programs. All of these concerns and more will be discussed in great detail in the chapters that follow. The higher the level of baseball you coach, the more you should know about the intricacies of the game and how to break down and teach skills. Head coaches must shoulder a lot of responsibility.

Baseball requires the ability to deal with failure that is built into the basic fabric of the game. Winning coaches must also begin to use the game to teach valuable life lessons. Often the first tough lesson we learn as a player or coach is "life is not fair." I can't think of any other game that relates to life as directly as the game of baseball.

The fundamental skills of correctly throwing, hitting, catching the ball, fielding, baserunning, pitching, and imparting game situations and the rules are vital to developing talented players and teams. Winning becomes the ultimate goal when we get to competitive, high-level youth baseball tournaments and high school baseball. The basic skill level of those older children should allow for very competitive games. However, games should never be won at the expense of a player being put at risk of personal injury by a coach.

A coach who runs a planned, organized practice can get a tremendous amount from his team. The players will look forward to his or her practices and have a great time playing baseball. Conversely, a coach who is always negative, yells and screams all the time, and/or does not run a competent practice can destroy a young person's baseball experience.

Unfortunately, this can turn kids away from the game forever. Every coach is responsible for keeping the game enjoyable for his or her players.

These days, it seems that most people fall into one of two extremes when it comes to coaching and parenting baseball players. They are either satisfied with being average, or they have lost all perspective and think only about winning and turning their child into the next Major Leaguer. To be a winning coach, you must not fall victim to either way of thinking. You will get a head start on being a winning coach or winning parent if you keep your perspective on what amateur baseball is all about. Just think how enjoyable the experience would be for kids of all ages if every coach and parent adhered to the goal to make their time with the children meaningful and rewarding.

PART ONE

Minimum Skill Expectation

The phrase "minimum skill expectation" means that by the time a player graduates from a particular baseball age group (T-ball, coach-pitch/ machine-pitch, or player-pitch), he or she can reasonably be expected to comprehend and perform the physical and mental baseball skills needed to be successful at that level. Thus, it is important that players grow up and advance through a baseball system (a league or series of teams) that emphasizes teaching developmentally appropriate physical and mental skills.

HOW DOES MINIMUM SKILL EXPECTATION WORK?

Coaches, parents, and players should focus on the essential offensive and defensive skills needed to be successful for the child's age group. In the following three chapters, each offensive

and defensive baseball skill is broken down into the basic components that are necessary to become a fundamentally sound player. When a player graduates from that particular age group, he or she should be able to perform the skills successfully on a consistent basis. This will give every player the greatest chance of having success at the next level of baseball. The old adage, *A picture is worth one thousand words,* has never been more true. Text is not the most effective way to demonstrate motion, team play, techniques, and all the other skills required to be a good baseball player. Follow the photos to understand the key movement components, and then watch the exercises and demonstrations on the DVD. The video will be your best guide to teaching and learning.

CHOOSE THE RIGHT EQUIPMENT FOR EARLY SUCCESS

When you watch T-ball, and coach/machine-pitch games, you are likely to see all types and sizes of gloves and bats. In a sport where the failure rate is already alarmingly high, the goal is to create situations where players will be successful. One thing that parents have control over is the size of the glove and bat their child uses.

Be sure to select a fielder's glove for your child that allows some margin for error. It is also a good idea if the glove is broken in. A modest-sized glove, such as one a teenaged second baseman uses, should be a good size for most young players. Be sure the glove is not too large: that it does not fall off a player's hand or that the small fingers can't sufficiently close the glove to hold the ball once it enters. Smaller fielder gloves can often be found in the garages or basements of your friends and neighbors—just ask them. Secondhand sports stores often stock used gloves you can purchase. This gives the fielder a chance for success because the ball can easily fit in the glove. The glove should almost close on its own when the ball enters. Some store-bought gloves are so small and stiff that the little fielder has to make a perfect catch. The glove may be cute but it will not be functional.

When choosing a bat, be sure not to purchase one that is too big. T-ball bats are relatively inexpensive and can be found in most department or sporting goods stores. At the T-ball level, players must be able to control the bat and swing it hard. Most T-ball bats don't have big barrels like those that are allowed at higher levels of baseball. Coach- or machine-pitch bats are significantly more expensive than T-ball bats and are not as easily found at department stores. Players can still choose to use a T-ball bat at this level, but they will eventually graduate to a bat that is higher-quality aluminum. Lightweight bats with the largest barrel allowed by the league, yet not too long, are usually the best choices. Often a player can try other team members' bats before deciding on their own.

Many players have their own personal batter's helmets to avoid transmitting hair fungi. Be sure the helmet is NOCSEE-approved (a helmet testing company) and fits snugly. A solid-color helmet that matches the team color is perfect. Black helmets can be worn year after year and may provide a few years use before players grow out of them.

Remember, it is important to set goals, but it is vital that those goals are truly the players' and not the parents' goals for their kids. It is also critical that players and parents keep the game and the player's ability level in perspective. The most important part of baseball is to have fun. It is a game and should never be treated like a job.

CHAPTER 1

MINIMUM SKILL EXPECTATION FOR T-BALL (Ages 4–6)

Myth #1: ALL CHILDREN WHO WANT TO PLAY BASEBALL MUST START AT THE T-BALL LEVEL.

Secret: *T-ball is the lowest level of baseball. It is for kids who show interest in playing this sport at a very young age. However, it is not absolutely necessary that kids start their baseball experience in T-ball. You can wait until they're a little bit older.*

Myth #2: THE BEST PLAYERS AT THE T-BALL LEVEL WILL EVENTUALLY BECOME THE BEST PLAYERS IN HIGH SCHOOL, COLLEGE, OR PROFESSIONAL BASEBALL.

Secret: *T-ball is entry-level baseball. Kids who show promise at this age may end up being advanced at older ages, but, in many cases, players who are less advanced at this age end up as good as or better than many of their more advanced contemporaries.*

Myth #3: WINNING MATTERS.

Secret: *Winning does not matter at the T-ball level. The only thing that really matters is that players learn a few basic skills while having fun. At this age, kids get excited over little victories such as making a catch, throwing the ball, getting on base, or scoring a run. Celebrate the small things and don't fall into the trap of worrying about the score.*

T-ball is the entry-level for the game of baseball. It is the age at which many kids in America get their first experience with this great game. Parents should exercise caution and avoid prematurely rushing their child into T-ball. Some children are not mentally, socially, or physically ready to start organized baseball at the age of four, five, or even six. Pushing your child to play organized baseball before he or she is ready could ultimately be detrimental and steer him or her away from the game forever. However, if your child shows an interest in baseball, enjoys the game, and does well following directions and working with other children, then it could be a good time to start his or her baseball experience.

The ultimate goal of every T-ball coach should be to make sure that each player is taught the very basic skills of the game. By its nature, baseball requires advanced gross and fine motor skills (large and small muscle movements), superior hand-eye coordination, and strong decision-making skills. These abilities are just starting to develop in the little bodies and minds of these players. Therefore, it is vital that coaches and parents begin very simply and stay at a simple level while a child is in T-ball. Just making a catch, a good throw, or solid contact with the baseball through a decent swing can be very rewarding for these young players. Celebrate with them and reinforce the positives whenever possible. The biggest challenge all T-ball coaches face is to capture the interest of their very young participants and make the game fun. The more success and fun kids have in practice and games, the more likely it is that they will stay with baseball for years to come. We need to make learning fun!

Coaches must focus the bulk of their allotted practice time on the fundamental skills of throwing, catching, fielding, hitting, and game situations. With the help of a few parents, coaches should set up simple stations where they spend no more than 10 minutes on each skill. Coaches and parents should use simple fun "picture words" to describe the skill action. Be energetic, encouraging, and reinforce any positive attributes you can find in each player. Give high-fives, smile, laugh, and show your players you care about them.

FUNDAMENTAL DEFENSE SKILLS FOR T-BALL

The focus of T-ball is to introduce and practice the most basic fundamental defensive skills of the game. This includes teaching defensive concepts and developing correct muscle memory, as well as cooperation skills with teammates. While offensive skills such as hitting and running the bases are what young players look forward to learning, defensive skills such as throwing, catching, fielding a ground ball, catching a fly ball, and comprehending simple game situations are vital to successfully playing baseball. As players progress to higher levels, defensive skills will become more important and will be needed in order to win games . . . when winning matters.

THROWING THE BALL

The game of baseball quickly transforms into a circus when players can't throw. Throwing is one of the most basic skills needed to play the game. Therefore, coaches and parents must spend concentrated practice time helping their players to become better throwers. The biggest challenge coaches will face with this age group is getting the youngsters to step towards their target correctly, getting into a good power position, and following through to complete the throw. In order to reduce fear and increase confidence, it's best to use very soft baseballs when T-ball players are learning to throw.

 Refer to T-Ball (Ages 4–6) "Throwing Mechanics" on the DVD for detailed interactive instruction.

The following minimum skill progression is needed for a T-ball player to throw a ball.

Grip
Because players this age have small hands, teach them to use three fingers for a proper grip to give them more control of the ball **(Figure 1.1)**.

Direction
Instruct the players to turn perpendicular to their target to improve direction and gain momentum. Simultaneously, they should step in opposition towards the target (i.e. a right-handed thrower steps with the left foot) to move the body into a good throwing position **(Figure 1.2)**.

Power Position
The player's eyes should be focused on the target. The front or glove-side elbow should be approximately shoulder-high and pointed at the target. The back or throwing-side elbow should also be approximately shoulder-

FIGURE 1.1

Teach these young players to hold the baseball with the proper grip using three fingers.

high, in a backwards "L" position, and pointed away from the target. The ball should be gripped correctly and pointed away from the target. The bottom half of the body should be in a good athletic position—feet wider than shoulders, knees slightly bent, and hips slightly flexed **(Figure 1.3)**.

Throw the Ball

To throw, the player accelerates the baseball from behind his or her body to a point out in front of the body where it is released towards the target. The throwing elbow should remain close to shoulder-high until the ball is released. A correct release of the ball should result in backwards spin, creating a twelve-o'clock to six-o'clock rotation **(Figure 1.4)**.

FIGURE 1.2

Players should turn the throwing-side foot sideways while stepping towards the target to gain momentum, establish good direction, and increase accuracy.

FIGURE 1.3

Teach players to create a good "power" position to get ready to throw.

FIGURE 1.4

Show players how to get good extension towards the target when making a throw.

FIGURE 1.5

Teach players to follow through once the ball is released.

Follow Through

Once the ball is released towards the target, the player should allow the throwing arm to decelerate naturally and finish just outside the stride-foot knee. The back foot will raise heel to the sky (to allow the hips to rotate), eventually lift off the ground, and finish slightly forward towards the target **(Figure 1.5)**.

Work through the following throwing drills and practice ideas to reinforce good throwing mechanics.

Specific Throwing Drills

 Refer to T-Ball (Ages 4–6) "Throwing Drills" on the DVD for the following drills:

A. Sitting wrist flip—Improves correct rotation of the ball at release.
B. Standing power position—Improves body direction and throwing posture.

Additional Throwing Practice
A. Instruct players to throw the ball hard to a coach, parent, or at a wall to eliminate the thinking process. This allows the throw to happen naturally and removes any fear that the player will hurt a throwing partner with the ball.
B. As players' throwing and catching abilities improve, allow them to play catch with a teammate. Pair up your better throwers and catchers with each other to help reduce fear, avoid injury, and increase repetitions.

CATCHING THE BASEBALL

It is common at this age for participants to have great difficulty making a clean catch. Because a baseball can come at them so many ways (hard or soft, directly at them or to the side, in front of them or behind them, in the air or on the ground), they will struggle to make the correct decision about how to position their glove to catch the ball without getting hurt. Coaches and parents should create simple, controlled stations where they throw to stationary players the same way every time, allowing the T-baller to work on the same type of catch. Celebrate and reinforce any catch that is made successfully along with the good attempts. In order to reduce fear and increase confidence in this age group, it is best to use tennis balls, Wiffle balls, or soft baseballs when players are learning to catch.

 Refer to T-Ball (Ages 4–6) "Catching the Ball" on the DVD for detailed interactive instruction.

The following minimum skill progression is needed for T-ball players to catch a ball thrown or hit to them in the air.

Above-the-Belt Catch
Instruct players to catch the ball with fingers up (towards the sky) when receiving balls thrown or batted above the belt. This puts the glove in the best position for the proper catch **(Figure 1.6)**.

Below-the-Belt Catch
Instruct players to catch the ball with fingers down (towards the ground) when receiving balls thrown or batted below the belt. This puts the glove

FIGURE 1.6

Show players how to catch the ball with fingers up to receive a ball above the belt.

FIGURE 1.7

Players should catch a below-the-belt ball with fingers down.

in the best position for the proper catch **(Figure 1.7)**.

Backhand Catch (Advanced Skill for T-Ball)

A backhanded catch is advanced for a T-ball player who typically will struggle catching the baseball in any way. The player should move his or her glove across the front of their body, directing the thumb towards the ground. This puts the glove in the best position to receive the baseball **(Figure 1.8)**.

FIGURE 1.8

Teach players to make a backhand catch by moving the glove across the body.

Work through the following drills and practice ideas to reinforce good catching mechanics.

Specific Catching Drills

A. Stationary glove side catch—Improves the confidence and catching ability for a ball thrown or batted to the glove side. Ask the player to stand still with the glove out to his or her side. Move close to the player and gently toss the ball underhanded directly to the glove. This removes the decision-making element of where to place the glove to make the catch, and it will improve confidence.

Additional Catching Practice

A. Coaches can throw to players at a catching drill station. This allows the coaches to focus on throwing to the player's glove in order to build up the child's confidence. Once players have improved enough to make simple catches, they can throw with partners who are at a similar ability level.

B. Advanced: Ask players to place their glove to the backhand side, and then throw the ball to the glove. Show them how to secure a successfully caught ball in the glove by placing their throwing hand over the ball.

FIELDING GROUND BALLS

Fielding balls hit on the ground requires a set of critical catching skills that should be learned and practiced early by all T-ball players. These include how to handle simple ground balls hit at the player or hit a short distance to either side. When a player graduates from T-ball, he or she should be able to execute basic ground ball mechanics and make throws to complete a force out at first and second base. To reduce fear, it's best to use tennis balls or very soft baseballs when T-ball players are learning to catch batted balls on the ground.

 Refer to T-Ball (Ages 4–6) "Fielding a Ground Ball (Infield)" on the DVD for detailed interactive instruction.

The following minimum skill progression is needed for a T-ball player to field a ground ball.

Ready Position

To be ready to move to a possible batted ball, instruct fielders to get into an athletic position before the hitter swings—feet wider than shoulders, knees slightly bent, hips slightly flexed, weight slightly forward, glove out with the pocket facing the batter, and eyes on the batting tee **(Figure 1.9)**.

Charge the Ball

When players see the baseball hit on the ground in their direction, they must take steps towards the ball ("charge the ball") under control to improve their position to field it, and to throw it to a base for an out **(Figure 1.10)**.

Fielding Position

Players should create a good fielding position by widening their feet outside their shoulders, bending their knees and hips, and lowering their upper body and glove to the ball. Tell your player to set the trap (glove) for the mouse (ball). The fingertips of the glove should rest on the ground

FIGURE 1.9

Teach players how to get into a ready position in order to move quickly to a batted ball.

FIGURE 1.10

Instruct fielders to move forward or to their side to get their body in front of a ground ball.

with the glove open to receive the baseball. The throwing hand should be above the glove (far enough from the glove to avoid being hit by a bad hop), ready to secure the ball in the glove and then quickly take the ball out to throw it. The head and eyes track the baseball into the glove for a catch **(Figure 1.11)**.

Power Position

The player takes the ball out of his or her glove while moving their feet and body sideways to the target to create a good power position or throwing position. The front shoulder, front elbow, side of front hip, and front toe should all end up pointed at the target, and the player is now ready to throw the ball **(Figure 1.12)**.

Throw the Ball

To make a throw, the player accelerates the baseball from behind the back shoulder and releases the ball in front of his or her body towards the target. The throwing elbow should remain close to shoulder-high until the

FIGURE 1.11

Show players how to create a good fielding position to catch a ground ball.

FIGURE 1.12

Instruct players to move into a good power position to increase throwing accuracy.

FIGURE 1.13

Players should create good extension toward the target when making a throw.

FIGURE 1.14

To finish the throwing process, instruct players to follow through once the ball is released.

ball is released. A correct release of the ball should result in a backwards spin, creating a twelve-o'clock to six-o'clock rotation **(Figure 1.13)**.

Follow Through

Once the ball is released towards the target, the player should allow his or her throwing arm to decelerate naturally and finish just outside the stride foot knee. The back foot will raise heel to the sky to allow the hips to rotate, and eventually lift off the ground and finish forward towards the target **(Figure 1.14)**.

Work through the following drills and practice ideas to reinforce good fielding mechanics.

Specific Ground Ball Drills

A. Stationary fielding position—Improves the confidence of a player to create a good fielding position and catch the ball with two hands. Softly roll the balls at fielders and encourage them to stay in front of the ball, field it, and throw it to a coach at a base.

15

B. Skateboard power position—Improves a player's transition of the ball from the glove to the hand as well as their throwing position before making a throw to a base. Ask players to start with the ball in their glove in a good fielding position. When you say "jump on the skateboard," the player transitions his or her feet perpendicular to their target like they are standing on a skateboard. They are now ready to throw the ball.

Additional Ground Ball Practice

A. Roll or softly hit balls to the glove side and encourage players to move their feet, field the ball in front, and throw the ball to a coach at a base.
B. Roll or softly hit balls to the throwing side and encourage players to move their feet, field the ball in front, and throw the ball to a coach at a base.
C. Roll or softly hit balls 10 feet to either side of the players, encouraging them to use their feet to get in front of the ball and then throw it to a coach at a base.
D. Roll balls to the player's side and instruct him or her to move to make the play, throw the ball back to you, and quickly release the ball to the other side for him or her to field. Continue the process for four repetitions.

FORCE OUTS AT FIRST BASE

Most T-ball players are not yet skilled enough to consistently catch a thrown or batted ball, so it is very difficult for them to play specific defensive positions. First base is a key position that should be reserved for one of the better catchers (receivers) on the team. The whole game of baseball starts with simple force outs at first base. It will improve the team's overall confidence if the player at first base has a chance to make a catch when the ball is thrown to him or her. At the T-ball level, catching skills are so poor that it is common for an entire offensive team to bat through the lineup without the defense recording a single out from a ball thrown to first base. To reduce fear, it's best to use tennis balls or very soft baseballs when T-ball players are learning to catch thrown balls.

The following minimum skill progression is needed for a T-ball player to catch a ball thrown to first base for a force out.

Footwork at the Base

Instruct the first baseman to place both heels on the side of the base parallel to the foul line and square his or her body to the person throwing the ball. The player should be relaxed and ready to react to a bad throw. A T-ball first baseman should use a larger glove that allows for a margin of error when catching the ball **(Figure 1.15)**.

Stretch for the Ball

When the baseball is in the air close to first base, instruct the player to stride (stretch) with his or her glove-side foot to meet the baseball, keeping the throwing-side foot on the side of the base for the force out **(Figure 1.16)**.

FIGURE 1.15

Instruct the first baseman to place both heels on the side of the base so there is a safe distance for the runner to cross the base without a collision.

FIGURE 1.16

If players see that the approaching ball is on target, they should stretch and catch the ball to make the force out.

Work through the following first base drills and practice ideas to reinforce good throwing mechanics.

Specific First Base Drills

A. Stationary receiving position—Improves the foot position on the base and the stretch for the ball. Start the first baseman with both heels on the base. Make simple throws and direct the player to stretch directly to the ball to make the catch. Vary your position around the infield when throwing.

B. Focus-on-the-base drill—Improves a first baseman's confidence to get to the base and set up without looking at the fielder making the play. Instruct the first baseman to start at his or her defensive position, about 5 to 10 feet away from the base and, on your command, to run to first base without looking at you or anyone else. The player should set up on the base (placing heels on the side of the base) while the coach yells out a position in the infield. The player must square his or her shoulders to face the stated position.

Additional First Base Practice

A. Hit or roll slow ground balls to the first baseman and ask him or her to run to first base to touch the base for the unassisted force out (the fielder makes the play and then touches the base by himself or herself).

B. A coach or parent can make random bad throws away from first base so fielders will learn to come off the base to stop the bad throw from getting past them. If they stop the ball and the base runner has not touched first base, teach them to tag the base runner or quickly touch first base before the base runner gets there.

FIELDING FLY BALLS

Successfully catching a fly ball is a significant challenge for a T-ball player. As mentioned earlier, routinely catching a thrown ball is difficult enough at this age level. However, coaches and parents must introduce this fundamental skill. It is important to practice this regularly in order for players to develop the hand-eye coordination and confidence needed to catch balls hit in the air to the infield or outfield. In order to reduce fear and improve confidence, it's best to use tennis balls, Wiffle balls, or very soft baseballs when T-ball players are learning to catch fly balls.

Refer to T-Ball (Ages 4–6) "Fielding a Fly Ball (Outfield)" on the DVD for detailed interactive instruction.

The following minimum skills progression is needed for a T-ball player to catch fly balls.

Ready Position

To be ready to move to a possible batted ball, instruct fielders to get into an athletic position (feet wider than shoulders, knees slightly bent, hips slightly flexed, weight slightly forward, glove out with the pocket facing the batter, and eyes on the batting tee) before the hitter swings **(Figure 1.17)**.

Move to the Ball

When fielders see the ball in the air, they must judge where it will come down. They must move their body to the baseball to catch it with two hands in front of them **(Figure 1.18)**.

FIGURE 1.17

Teach players to get into a ready position in order to move quickly to a batted ball.

FIGURE 1.18

Instruct players to position their body in front of ball to prepare to make a catch.

Catch the Ball

Fielders must raise their glove in front of their head in anticipation of the ball, and open the glove to the ball. They should let the ball travel to the glove (instead of stabbing or jumping at it) and squeeze it firmly once it enters the glove. They should also place the throwing hand on top of the ball to keep it securely in the glove. Let players catch the ball on their glove side at first until they gain confidence. Then slowly encourage them to catch the ball in front of them **(Figure 1.19)**.

Power Position

Players take the ball out of their glove while moving their feet and body sideways to the target to create a good power position or throwing position. The front shoulder, elbow, toe, and side of the front hip should all end up pointed at the target, and the player is now ready to throw the ball **(Figure 1.20)**.

FIGURE 1.19

Instruct players to visually track the ball into their glove and secure the catch with two hands.

FIGURE 1.20

Teach players to move their body into a good power position to increase throwing accuracy.

FIGURE 1.21

Show players how to get good extension towards the target when making a throw.

FIGURE 1.22

To finish the throwing process, teach players to follow through once the ball is released.

Throw the Ball

To make a throw, the player accelerates the baseball from behind his or her body to a point in front of the body to release it towards the target. The throwing elbow should remain close to shoulder-high until the ball is released. Correctly releasing the ball should result in a backwards spin, creating a twelve-o'clock to six-o'clock rotation **(Figure 1.21)**.

Follow Through

Once the ball is released towards the target, the player should allow his or her throwing arm to decelerate naturally and finish just outside the stride-foot knee. The back foot will raise heel to the sky to allow the hips to rotate, and eventually lift off the ground and finish forward towards the target **(Figure 1.22)**.

Work through the following drills and practice ideas to reinforce good fly ball mechanics.

Specific Fly Ball Drills

 Refer to T-Ball (Ages 4–6) "Outfield Drills" on the DVD for the following drill:

A. Tennis racket drill—Improves the confidence of a player moving to a fly ball and catching it.

Additional Fly Ball Practice

A. Gently throw or softly hit fly balls to the fielder's glove side.
B. Gently throw or softly hit fly balls directly to the fielder.
C. Gently toss the ball, leading the player to the glove side so he or she can catch fly balls on the run.

FUNDAMENTAL OFFENSE SKILLS FOR T-BALL

In T-ball, "offense" skills encompass hitting and simple baserunning. At this level of the game, players need to learn how to address a batting tee with a correct setup, hold the bat with a proper grip, create a basic stance, swing the bat aggressively, get their back heel to rotate off the ground, and run to the proper base when a ball is hit. Don't assume that players will know when or what base to run to. It is common to see a T-ball player hit the ball and run to third base thinking he or she is going in the right direction or cut right across the pitcher's mound when running from first to third base, skipping second base on the way!

The goal is to keep swing mechanics very simple to give players the greatest chance of consistently hitting the ball hard. Don't give a young player too many things to think about at one time. This can significantly slow the learning process and lead to frustration. Remember to celebrate the small successes such as taking a good swing, even if the player completely misses the ball.

This section of offense will focus primarily on hitting. Simple baserunning situations that should be taught in practice or reinforced in games will be covered in the "Coaching T-Ball 101: Teaching Game Skills" section at the end of this chapter.

 Refer to T-Ball (Ages 4–6) "Hitting Mechanics" on the DVD for detailed interactive instruction.

The following is the minimum skill expectation for a T-ball player to swing the bat.

Setup

It is very important to assure correct tee placement for the hitter to have the greatest chance of solid contact with the ball. Ideally, players should hit the ball on the "sweet spot," "fat part," or "barrel" of the bat when they swing. If they are too far away or too close to the batting tee, the player is set up to fail before taking a swing. The ball should be resting on the batting tee between mid-thigh and belt high **(Figure 1.23)**.

Proper Grip

Pay particularly close attention to the player's basic grip of the bat. With a correct grip, the door-knocking knuckles should be close to lined up. A poor grip can cause serious swing flaws that will inhibit consistent solid contact with the ball and frustrate the hitter **(Figure 1.24)**.

FIGURE 1.23

Check your hitters for proper distance from the batting tee to allow the best chance for the barrel of the bat to hit the ball.

FIGURE 1.24

Check your hitters for a correct grip, which will help create a proper swing.

FIGURE 1.25

Set up your player at the batting tee so he or she can swing the bat hard and hit the ball off the barrel of the bat.

FIGURE 1.26

Encourage the player to take a short stride and attack the baseball while keeping both hands on the bat throughout the swing.

FIGURE 1.27

Teach the player to finish a swing with the bat shoulder-high and the back foot in a "heel to sky" position.

Batting Stance

To ensure a correct starting position for the player's hands, show him or her how to place the bat on their back shoulder and then lift the bat off the shoulder six inches or so. The hitter's bottom hand (knob hand) should start near the height of the back shoulder. The feet should be wider apart than shoulder width, and the hitter should feel balanced (Figure 1.25).

Contact with the Ball

Ideally, the player's hands should be in a palm up/palm down (top hand palm up and bottom hand palm down) relationship when the bat makes contact with the baseball. This will give the hitter the best chance to hit the ball hard. The hitter's back heel should start to rotate off the ground. Teach your players to take an aggressive swing at the ball **(Figure 1.26)**.

Swing Finish

At the conclusion of the swing, the bat should finish as high as the front shoulder. Place emphasis on the back foot, making sure the heel is rotated to the sky to allow the hips to work freely and provide more power to the hitter. The goal is to be able to swing hard and stay balanced. A hitter should not spin in a circle or fall over the plate after completing a correct swing **(Figure1.27)**.

Work through the following hitting drills and practice ideas to reinforce good hitting mechanics.

Specific Hitting Drills

 Refer to T-Ball (Ages 4–6) "Hitting Drills" on the DVD for the following drill:

A. Basic tee drill—Improves overall setup at the tee and swing of a hitter.

Additional Hitting Practice

A. Hit for distance—Set up tees with Wiffle or tennis balls and see who can hit the farthest. This encourages players to take full swings and attack the baseball.
B. Practice proper setup to the tee—Create a practice station where players are taught how to set up in relationship to the tee to learn good plate coverage for the swing.
C. Focus on a back "heel to the sky" finish—Ask players to hit a tennis ball off the tee into a fence. Their back heel must end up pointed to the sky to ensure they are using the lower half of their body to swing. The hips provide power and are released when the back heel lifts off the ground, leaving the tip of the toe in contact with the ground.

COACHING T-BALL 101: TEACHING GAME SKILLS

For a successful T-ball game, coaches must not only teach the fundamental skills of throwing, catching, fielding, and hitting, they must prepare their players for basic situations that will arise when competing against another team. Below is a simple list of offensive and defensive team skills or basic situations that should be mastered by the time a player graduates T-ball. Use practice time and games to reinforce these skills.

Team Offense—The Basics

Teach your players the following:

1. How to hit the ball and run to the correct base.
2. How to run through first base (this is the only base besides home where this is allowed).
3. How to run to other bases and know which base to run to next by listening and following the directions of their base coaches.
4. That they should listen to the team base coaches only and not to parents screaming from the stands or next to the fence.
5. Advanced: How to slide feet-first into all bases except for first base.
6. Advanced: How to return to their original base when a ball is caught in the air with less than two outs.

Note: In T-ball games, coaches should avoid the temptation to play "cat and mouse" with their base runners to cause chaos with the defense. This eats up valuable time and takes away from the opportunity to learn basic game skills that must be mastered by the players to move to higher levels of the game.

Coaches must keep order, organization, and safety in the dugout. This is a great job to assign to a "team mom" or "team dad" so the coaches can concentrate on teaching the game.

Team Defense—The Basics

Teach your players the following:

1. Where to stand in the field to play their specific position.
2. How to make force outs at first base.
3. How to make force outs at all other bases.
4. How to create outs by tagging base runners.
5. How to properly communicate on fly balls by calling for the ball. This will reduce collisions and increase confidence to make the catch.

6. Where to throw the ball when it goes into the outfield.

7. How to stop the play (create a "dead ball"). Each league has different rules for ending a play at this level.

POST-GAME TALK

At the conclusion of each game, the coach should bring the team together into a group in the outfield or just outside the field of play. This should be done without the parents of the players gathering around the team, which can distract the children. The coach should review some of the simple things that were learned from playing that game.

- The coach should talk positively about the game: don't emphasize winning or losing or single out any player. Keep the summary short and sweet.
- The coach should remind players of the next practice or game even though most players won't remember. This teaches responsibility; players will need this skill as they grow older.
- The coach should bring the team together for a simultaneous dismissal where all players put their hands together and shout "Team!"

The coach should have arranged for parents to bring a team snack or drink to provide after each post-game talk.

Refer to Chapter 8, "Coaching Youth Baseball," for more ideas on how to conduct a productive and enjoyable baseball practice.

CHAPTER 2

MINIMUM SKILL EXPECTATION FOR COACH-PITCH/ MACHINE-PITCH BASEBALL (Ages 7–8)

Myth #1: BECAUSE OF THE WAY THE BALL SHOOTS OUT OF A MACHINE, COACH-PITCH BASEBALL IS BETTER FOR CHILDREN THAN MACHINE-PITCH.

Secret: *Neither coach-pitch nor machine-pitch is better than the other. What is best depends on the child, the coach, and the machine. At this age level, the most important element is that players get used to hitting a moving baseball. Some coaches throw well and give their players the confidence to hit off a live pitcher; other coaches may not have the control to throw strikes at just the right speed for the hitter to be successful. Machines have their own set of difficulties including inconsistency and unrealistic release (compared to an arm). They can also be dangerous in bad weather, and they can be expensive.*

Myth #2: PLAYERS MUST BE ABLE TO HIT A MOVING BASEBALL TO BE SIGNED UP FOR COACH-PITCH OR MACHINE-PITCH BASEBALL.

Secret: *At this level, it is the coach's duty to give the player the confidence to hit a moving baseball by providing instruction and drills. A player generally has two years at this level to learn to hit a baseball pitched by a player.*

Myth #3: WINNING MATTERS.

Secret: *Winning does not matter at this level; it is most important to provide a positive experience for the players. They should learn how to execute the basic skills of the game. Does anyone remember or care about the record of his/ her coach-pitch or machine-pitch team? I hope not.*

Coach-pitch/machine-pitch baseball is typically the second tier of organized baseball. It provides new opportunities to reinforce and further develop fundamental skills needed to play the game correctly. At this level, the ball is pitched to the batter, instead of players hitting the stationary ball of T-ball. The catcher position has also been added.

Hitting a moving baseball with consistent skill is arguably the hardest thing to do in all of sports. The muscular strength, hand-eye coordination, and confidence needed to make regular contact with a moving ball are difficult for players of this age to master. Therefore, a major focus in coach-pitch or machine-pitch baseball should be to improve a player's hitting ability, while building dexterity and confidence. This will provide players with an offensive foundation to take their game to the next level, in which they will have to hit pitches from players their own age.

Compared to T-ball, at this age level more attention will be paid to specific components of the biomechanics of defensive skills, along with additional drills to reinforce correct muscle memory. The key objective is for coaches and parents to make sure each defensive skill is being performed at a developmentally appropriate level.

Coaches are challenged to make practices and games fun for the kids. This can be accomplished if coaches are willing to learn how to teach the skills and drills, as well as put some planning into practice. Coaches must also stay positive and encourage the players at all times. With the help of a few parents, coaches should set up simple stations in practice where they spend no more than 10 to 15 minutes on each skill. Otherwise children will be left standing around and will grow bored.

This level of baseball often lacks the constant action and stimulation that kids love, enjoy, and find in other sports. Baseball has short bursts of action followed by thinking, and it is hard for young minds to appreciate the game for what it is. Because many hitters struggle to make contact with the ball, children may find themselves standing around a lot of the time during a game. Young participants may drop out of baseball at this level because of the high rate of failure when trying to hit, fear of getting hit with a moving pitch, overbearing coaches or parents, and lack of action or fun in practices and games.

The tendency is for some coaches or parents to try to give the players too much information in an honest attempt to improve their skills or advance them beyond their peers. Too much information can be just as dangerous as too little information in the development of a coach-pitch/machine-pitch player. Parents must fight the trend to drive their child to be the best in hopes that one day he or she will become a Major League player.

FUNDAMENTAL DEFENSE SKILLS
FOR COACH-PITCH/MACHINE-PITCH

At this level, it is still a big challenge for players to accurately throw, consistently catch, and routinely field the ball on the ground and in the air. Because of variables such as the speed, height, and distance of thrown or batted balls, poor field conditions, and various game situations, it is important to use practice time to reduce the exterior variables. Skills and drills need to be simplified in order to increase the success rates of participants. For example, instead of hitting random ground balls to all the infielders, roll ground balls to the same infield position repeatedly so players can concentrate on using the correct fielding mechanics they were taught in the drills. As players gradually improve their defensive fundamentals, they will become more consistent, more confident, and have more fun playing the game.

THROWING THE BALL

Throwing is the most fundamental defensive skill in baseball. It is needed to successfully play every defensive position on the field. If a player can't consistently throw the ball to an intended target, he or she will quickly become discouraged and lose confidence. Poor throwers may eventually distance themselves from the game of baseball altogether. Participants who have graduated from T-ball may have a little more experience throwing, but typically most players at this age continue to struggle with consistent mechanics and accuracy.

Coaches should implement throwing drills at the start of every practice and before every game. Parents should also take time to learn the age-appropriate throwing drills to teach their child, and use them whenever they play catch. This will help players develop correct throwing mechanics. Emphasis should be placed on the player using a proper grip, executing a correct power position, and finishing the throw.

 Refer to Coach-/Machine-Pitch (Ages 7–8) "Throwing Mechanics" on the DVD for detailed interactive instruction.

The following is the minimum skill progression needed for a coach-pitch or machine-pitch player to throw a ball.

Grip

Give players the choice of using two or three fingers for a proper grip around the ball. Emphasize proper thumb placement on the bottom of the ball while making sure the player does not squeeze the ball too tightly **(Figure 2.1)**.

Teach players to recognize a four-seam grip where they hold the ball with the pads of the top two or three fingers resting across the laces. This helps the ball travel straight when it is released correctly with backspin **(Figure 2.2)**.

FIGURE 2.1

Instruct players to hold the baseball with a relaxed grip, using two or three fingers on top of the ball and the thumb underneath the ball.

Momentum and Direction

Show players how to initiate direction to their target by turning their throwing-side foot perpendicular. This helps gain needed momentum while squaring the body into a power position **(Figure 2.3)**.

Power Position

The player's eyes should be focused on the target. The front (glove-side) elbow should be approximately shoulder-high and pointed directly at the target. The throwing elbow should also be approximately shoulder-high, creating a backwards "L", and it should be pointed away from the target.

FIGURE 2.2

Introduce a four-seam throwing grip, which is created by holding the ball across the seams.

FIGURE 2.3

Players should turn the throwing-side foot sideways while stepping towards the target to gain momentum, establish good direction, and increase accuracy.

The player should grip the ball correctly, with the wrist relaxed, pointed outward, and away from the target. The bottom half of the body should be in a good athletic position with the player's feet wider than his or her shoulders, knees slightly bent, and hips slightly flexed **(Figure 2.4)**.

Throwing the Ball

Instruct the player to accelerate the baseball from behind his or her body to a point out in front of the body where it is released towards the target. The throwing elbow should remain shoulder-high through release. This will help the player stay on top of and behind the ball when the throwing arm is completely extended towards the target. The player should snap the wrist to let go of the ball with backspin **(Figure 2.5)**.

Follow Through

Once the ball is released towards the target, the player should allow his or her throwing arm to decelerate naturally and finish just outside the stride-foot knee. The back shoulder should finish forward, pointed at the target. The back foot will raise heel to the sky, allowing the hips to rotate, and eventually lift off the ground and finish forward near the stride foot **(Figure 2.6)**.

FIGURE 2.4

Players should create a good power position in order to make an accurate throw.

FIGURE 2.5

The player should achieve good extension towards the target with the throwing arm.

Work through the following drills and practice ideas to reinforce good throwing mechanics.

Throwing Drills

 Refer to Coach-/Machine-Pitch (Ages 7–8) "Throwing Drills" on the DVD for the following drills:

A. Sitting wrist flip—Reinforces the proper throwing grip and improves rotation of the ball at release.
B. Standing power position—Reinforces a proper throwing position to improve accuracy.
C. Standing figure eight—Creates rhythm and tempo in the throwing process.

FIGURE 2.6

Once the ball is released, the player should follow through with the throwing arm.

Additional Throwing Practice

A. Instruct players to throw hard to a coach, parent, or against a wall to remove the thinking process. This allows the throw to happen naturally and removes the fear of hurting a throwing partner with the ball.
B. Once players are warmed up and finished with their throwing drills, they should throw for distance. Players should gradually extend their throws to a point where they make three to five throws as far as possible. This will help them use their whole body to throw the ball.
C. Set up fun targets on a fence, wall, or other safe area for players to throw at. Assign points to targets based on difficulty, and give a time limit to accomplish the throws. Setting a reasonable time limit for the throws will deter players from aiming the ball and force them to release the ball.

CATCHING THE BASEBALL

Catching is the sister skill to throwing a baseball—every ball that is thrown will usually be caught by another teammate. The inability to catch a ball will make playing the game of baseball difficult and, in most instances, dangerous. Every defensive position on the field should be working towards consistently catching thrown baseballs as well as those batted in the air and on the ground.

Coaches should implement drill stations in practice to teach and reinforce various catching skills. Because the skills of players will vary significantly at this age, the better players must continue to be challenged by coaches and parents or they will become bored with these catching stations. Use tennis balls or soft baseballs when players are first learning to catch. This will reduce fear and increase confidence, thus improving success rates. Always partner up the better throwers and catchers so they can relax and execute repetitions without fear of hurting each other. Players at this level should begin to show confidence when catching baseballs at a moderate speed, without moving out of the way.

 Refer to Coach-/Machine-Pitch (Ages 7–8) "Catching the Ball" on the DVD for detailed interactive instruction.

The following is the minimal skill progression needed for seven- and eight-year-old players to catch a ball thrown or batted in the air.

Above-the-Belt Catch

Teach players to catch baseballs thrown above the belt, line drives above the belt, or fly balls with their fingers up towards the sky. This puts the glove in the best position for the proper catch. Whenever possible, players should move their feet to catch the ball between their shoulders. However, some balls will be caught on a player's glove side or the backhand side due to the speed of the ball or the player's fear of being hit by the ball **(Figure 2.7)**.

Below-the-Belt Catch

Teach players to catch balls thrown below the belt, low line drives, and balls that bounce low to the ground with their fingers down towards the ground. This puts the glove in the best position for this type of catch **(Figure 2.8)**.

FIGURE 2.7

Teach players to receive the ball with fingers up to make a catch above the belt.

FIGURE 2.8

Teach players to receive a ball with fingers down to make a catch below the belt.

Backhand Catch

Teach players to catch the ball to the backhand side when they are not able to move their feet to catch the ball in front of their body. The player should move the glove across the front of the body, directing the thumb of the glove towards the ground. The player's hips should rotate slightly towards the ball, positioning the glove-side elbow where it is close to being pointed at the ball. This puts the glove in the proper position to make the catch **(Figure 2.9)**.

FIGURE 2.9

Teach players to receive a ball to the backhand side when there is no time to get in front of the thrown or batted ball.

Work through the following catching drills and practice ideas to reinforce good catching mechanics.

Specific Catching Drills

A. Stationary glove-side and front catch—Improves confidence and the ability to catch a ball thrown or batted to the glove side and directly at a player. First, instruct the player to stand still with his or her glove out to their side and then progress to catching between the shoulders. Start close to the player and gently toss the ball, underhand, directly to his or her glove, above and below the belt. Gradually increase distance and speed, progressing to an overhand throw as players demonstrate mastery.

B. Stationary backhand catch—Improves the confidence and catching ability for a ball thrown or batted to the backhand side. Instruct the player to stand stationary with his or her glove-side hip rotated towards the ball and their glove across the body to their backhand side. Start close to the player and gently toss the ball, underhand, directly to his or her glove, above and below the belt. Gradually increase distance and speed, progressing to an overhand throw as players demonstrate mastery.

Once players can consistently catch baseballs thrown to them, specific catching drills can be eliminated except for during throwing drills or when warming up to throw. Players will also use their catching skills at other drill stations, such as fielding fly balls in the outfield, playing an infield position, receiving throws at first base, or playing the catcher position.

Additional Catching Practice

A. Movement to the glove side—The player should jog or run slowly to his or her glove side as a coach gently leads the player with a throw meant to be caught.

B. Movement to the backhand side—The player should jog or run slowly to his or her throwing side as a coach gently leads the player with a throw meant to be caught with backhand mechanics.

C. Advanced: Moving backwards to make a catch—Instruct the player to move backwards away from the coach (instead of side to side or moving forward) to make a catch. Start by working the glove side and progress to a backhanded catch, which is the most difficult.

To make any of the previously mentioned catches more difficult, simply increase the speed, angle, and distance of the baseball to be caught.

FIELDING GROUND BALLS

Infielders and outfielders must all eventually possess the ability to consistently field ground balls, transition into a throwing position, and make accurate throws to bases. Once players recognize that the ball has been hit on the ground, they must move their body forward (or to the side) to be in a good position to field, and then transition into an effective power position to throw. The ball will be hit with varying speeds in various directions, and it may take erratic hops. Therefore, coaches and parents must allot adequate time in practice and at home to reinforce good fielding habits and drills so players can develop the confidence to field the ball off the ground. Use soft baseballs until players become comfortable staying in front of the ball and overcome the fear of being hit with a bad hop.

 Refer to Coach-/Machine-Pitch (Ages 7–8) "Fielding a Ground Ball (Infield)" on the DVD for detailed interactive instruction.

The following is the minimum skill progression needed for seven- and eight-year old players to field a ground ball.

Ready Position

To prepare to move to a batted ball, teach fielders to get into an athletic position (their legs should be spread wider than their shoulder width, knees slightly bent, hips slightly flexed, weight slightly forward, glove out in front of the body with the pocket facing the batter, and eyes on the hitter) before the batter swings **(Figure 2.10)**.

FIGURE 2.10

Teach fielders to get into a ready position so they can efficiently react to a batted ball.

Charge the Ball

Teach players to close in on a baseball batted in their direction by moving to the side or towards the ball. This puts the player in a better position to field the ball and creates more time to throw the base runner out **(Figure 2.11)**.

FIGURE 2.11

Teach players to charge the ground ball with control to get in front of it.

FIGURE 2.12

Teach players how to create a good fielding position to catch a ground ball.

Fielding Position

Players should create a good fielding position by increasing the distance between their legs to lower their upper body and bring the glove to the ground ball. The fingertips of the glove should be on the ground, at the top of an imaginary triangle created by the top of both feet and the mitt. The player should open the glove to receive the baseball, and close it once the ball enters. The throwing hand should be above the glove, ready to secure the ball in the glove, yet ready to quickly throw it. The player's head and eyes should follow the moving baseball into the glove for a catch **(Figure 2.12)**.

Power Position

As players take the ball out of their glove, they should turn their body side-ways towards the target base to create a good body position to throw while gaining some momentum. The ball itself should be behind their body, pointed away from the target in a relaxed grip. The back elbow should be approximately shoulder-high. The front shoulder, elbow, front hip, and front toe should all end up pointed at the target, and the player will be ready to throw the ball **(Figure 2.13)**.

FIGURE 2.13

In order for infielders to quickly and accurately throw to a base, they must be taught how to efficiently transition from a fielding position into a power position.

FIGURE 2.14

To make an accurate throw, the fielder should extend the throwing hand to the target.

Throw the Ball: Extension

The fielder should transition from the power position into the throw by accelerating the baseball from behind the back shoulder towards the target. The throwing elbow should stay at least shoulder-high until the ball is released. The fielder should fully extend the throwing hand to the target while the back shoulder moves forward to replace the front shoulder by ending up pointed at the target **(Figure 2.14)**.

FIGURE 2.15

To finish the throwing process, teach players to follow through once the ball is released

Follow Through

Once the ball is released towards the target, the player should allow his or her throwing arm to decelerate naturally and finish just outside the stride-foot knee. The back foot will raise heel to the sky (to allow the hips to rotate) and eventually lift off the ground and finish slightly forward towards the target **(Figure 2.15)**.

Work through the following drills and practice ideas to reinforce good fielding mechanics.

Specific Fielding Drills

A. Charge to fielding position—Improves the confidence of a player to charge the ball and create a good fielding position. Draw a fielding triangle created by the top of the feet and the glove, and place a stationary ball at the top. Back up the infielder 10 feet from the ball. On the command of the coach or a parent, the player should charge the ball under control and get into a good fielding position with his or her feet at the base of the triangle and the glove at the apex. Once a player can repeat a good approach into a fielding position, the coach or parent can add a rolling ball to increase difficulty.

B. Fielding position to power position—Improves a player's transition of the ball from the fielding position to a throwing position. Instruct players to start in a good fielding position, with the ball in their glove at the top of the fielding triangle. When you say "power," players quickly move their feet perpendicular to their target while taking the ball out of their glove, up into a good power position. They are now ready to throw the ball to their target.

Additional Ground Ball Practice

A. Place the player in a good fielding position with a ball in his or her glove. On the command of a coach or parent, the player must transition to throw the ball to the adult.

B. The player throws a tennis ball against a wall and quickly moves his or her feet to field the ball in a good position. This can be done with a glove or barehanded.

C. Coaches or parents roll or softly hit ground balls, moving infielders 10 feet to either side. Coach them to get in front of ball, create a good fielding position, power position, and throw to an adult at first base.

FORCE OUTS AT FIRST BASE

At the coach-pitch/machine-pitch level, first base is one of the most important defensive positions on the field since it is the most fundamental force out in the game of baseball. For example, infielders must be able to throw the ball to the first baseman, who will successfully catch it and touch the base before the runner gets there. The first baseman should be comfortable catching the ball to the glove side and backhand. It is a good idea to alternate at first base the players who possess the best catching skills.

The following is the minimum skill progression needed for seven- and eight-year-olds to play first base.

Footwork Around First Base

Teach the first baseman to move quickly to the base when the ball is hit to the infield. The player should place both heels on the side of first base parallel to the foul line to create a safe distance from the base runner. The fielder should square his or her body to face the person making the throw, stay relaxed, and be ready to stretch to a good throw or react to a bad throw **(Figure 2.16)**.

FIGURE 2.16

The first baseman must quickly get to the base, place both heels on the side of the base, and square his or her body to the person throwing the ball.

Stretch for the Ball

The first baseman should wait to see if the throw is on target before committing to stretch to catch the ball **(Figures 2.17, 2.18)**. When the thrown baseball is close to first base, the player must stride towards the ball with his or her glove-side foot, and reach with the glove to meet and receive the baseball. The first baseman must keep the throwing-side foot on the side of the base for the force out. If the throw is off-target, the first baseman should abandon the base to stop the ball from getting past him or her. Then he or she should attempt to tag the base runner before the runner reaches first base.

Work through the following drills and practice ideas to reinforce good first base mechanics.

FIGURE 2.17

This first baseman stretches with fingers up to receive a throw above the waist.

FIGURE 2.18

This first baseman stretches with fingers down to receive a throw below the waist.

Specific First Base Drills

A. Semicircle throws—Improves the confidence of a first baseman stretching to catch the ball thrown from all infield positions. Two players and a coach form a semicircle around first base from 20 feet away. They each should be in the general direction of an infield position (third base, shortstop, second base). All three feeders take turns throwing the ball to the player on first base, who stretches to make the catch and throws the ball back to the person who threw it.

B. Focus-on-the-base drill—Improves a first baseman's confidence to get to the base and set up without looking at the fielder making the play. Instruct the first baseman to start at his or her pre-pitch defensive position, and on your command, run to first base without looking at the coach or anyone else. This simulates the time the ball has been hit to another infielder. The player should quickly set up on first base while the coach yells out a specific position in the infield. The player then squares his or her shoulders to face the stated position as if to receive a throw from there.

Additional First Base Practice

A. Hit ground balls to the infield and instruct players to throw to first base to complete a force out.

B. Hit ground balls to the infield, and instruct base runners to run from home to first base while the defense attempts to complete a force out by throwing to the base before the runner gets there.

C. Time the fastest runners on your team from their swing at home plate to arriving at first base. Gauge whether fielders are receiving the ball, throwing the ball, and making the force out at first base in the time you recorded. The clock starts on contact with the bat and stops with the catch at first base.

OUTFIELD PLAY: CATCHING FLY BALLS

Many seven- and eight-year-old players will struggle to catch a ball hit in the air. Therefore, it is important to continue improving the hand-eye coordination needed to catch fly balls in both the outfield and the infield. At the start of the season, coaches and parents must focus on general catching skills, as discussed earlier in this chapter. As players improve their catching abilities, coaches and parents should begin to work on outfield as a specific defensive position with the preliminary focus on catching basic fly balls. Adults should create practice stations that simulate fly balls, which outfielders will attempt to catch in a game. In order to reduce fear and increase confidence, introduce drills using tennis balls or soft baseballs.

 Refer to Coach-/Machine-Pitch (Ages 7–8) "Fielding a Fly Ball (Outfield)" on the DVD for detailed interactive instruction.

The following is the minimum skill progression needed for a seven- and eight-year-old player to catch a fly ball in the outfield.

Ready Position

To be ready to move to a possible batted ball, instruct fielders to take small steps or "creep" into an athletic position (legs spread wider than shoulders, knees slightly bent, hips slightly flexed, weight slightly forward, glove out with the pocket facing forward, and eyes focused on the batter) before the hitter swings **(Figure 2.19)**.

FIGURE 2.19

Players can quickly move to batted fly ball from a ready position.

FIGURE 2.20

Instruct players to run softly as they get into position to make a catch.

Move to the Ball

When fielders see the ball in the air, they must judge where it will land and move to the baseball to catch it with two hands in front of them. Teach players to run softly on their feet to keep their head and eyes from moving up and down, which will create the illusion of the ball bouncing in the sky and make it harder to catch **(Figure 2.20)**.

Catch the Ball

To be in a position to receive the ball, fielders must raise their glove early above and directly in front of their head. The glove fingers should be pointed towards the sky. Teach players to let the ball travel to the glove (they should not stab or jump to make a catch) and to squeeze the ball firmly once it enters the glove. Players should place the throwing hand on top of the ball to keep it securely in the glove **(Figure 2.21)**.

Power Position

Players should take the ball out of their glove while moving their body forward into a power position. This allows them to use their legs in order to gain momentum towards the target. The front elbow, front hip, and front toe should all end up pointed at the target. The outfielder is now ready to throw

FIGURE 2.21

Teach players to secure the catch with two hands.

FIGURE 2.22

After the catch, the player should get into a good power position to throw the ball.

the ball. More advanced players can implement a small "crow hop" by driving their throwing-side foot forward to quickly gain momentum (**Figure 2.22**).

Throw the Ball

To make a throw, the player accelerates the baseball from behind his or her body to a point out in front of the body where it is released towards the target. The throwing elbow should remain close to shoulder-high until the ball is released in front of the body. Correctly releasing the ball should result in a backwards spin, creating a twelve-o'clock to six-o'clock rotation (**Figure 2.23**).

FIGURE 2.23

Teach outfielders to get good extension towards the target when making a throw.

Follow Through

Once the ball is released towards the target, the player should allow his or her throwing arm to decelerate naturally and finish just outside the knee of their stride foot. The back foot will raise heel to the sky (to allow the hips to rotate) and eventually lift off the ground and finish slightly forward towards the target **(Figure 2.24)**.

FIGURE 2.24

To complete the play, instruct the player to follow through once the ball is released.

Work through the following drills and practice ideas to reinforce good fly ball mechanics.

Specific Fly Ball Drills

 Refer to Coach-/Machine-Pitch (Ages 7–8) "Outfield Drills" on the DVD for the first drill below:

A. Tennis racket drill—Improves the confidence of a player moving to catch a fly ball.

B. Stationary crow hop drill—Improves an outfielder's ability to add momentum to the throw. Start outfielders with a ball in their glove above their head to simulate a caught fly ball. Make sure each player's throwing-side foot is back behind his or her body. On your command, they should drive their back foot towards the target to end in a power position.

Additional Fly Ball Practice

A. Throw or softly hit balls to the outfielder's glove side and backhand side. Encourage the player to get in front of the fly ball and catch it with the glove above his or her head and between the shoulders when possible.

B. Teach outfielders to run short, football-style patterns, leading them to catch the ball on the run. Emphasize running softly and to refrain from reaching to make the catch until the ball is near them. Use soft, textured baseballs or tennis balls to reduce fear.

To add difficulty to these drills, simply increase the height, distance, and speed of the ball.

THE CATCHER POSITION

In coach-pitch/machine-pitch baseball, the defensive position of catcher (the player who receives the pitched baseball from the coach or from a pitching machine) becomes more important in function. Some players interested in the position may decide they are not comfortable being close to a hitter swinging the bat, and others may instinctively close their eyes every time the hitter swings at a pitch. It is important to identify the right player for the catcher position so he or she will have the confidence to learn the basics.

For this age group, the best catchers will be children who receive the ball well (as discussed at the start of the chapter) but are also physically tough, for they are bound to be struck with foul tips and balls that bounce off the ground. If you don't have a player who can do a satisfactory job as the catcher, you may want to put a coach behind that player in the game to save time chasing down the baseball after every pitch.

 Refer to Coach-/Machine-Pitch (Ages 7–8) "The Catcher Position" on the DVD for detailed interactive instruction.

The following is the minimum skill progression needed for seven- and eight-year-olds to play the position of catcher.

Positioning to the Hitter

The coach should teach catchers how to create the proper distance from the hitter to protect them from being hit with a swung bat. They should be far enough from the hitter so they cannot reach out and touch the batter's back leg **(Figure 2.25)**.

The Basic Receiving Stance

Teach catchers to create a basic receiving stance with their knees bent, feet placed wider than their knees, toes pointed

FIGURE 2.25

The catcher must wear proper gear and create enough distance from the hitter to avoid getting hit with a bat.

47

FIGURE 2.26

Teach the catcher to use a basic receiving stance to catch a ball thrown from a coach or machine.

FIGURE 2.27

The catcher should extend the glove arm in front of the knees to receive a pitch.

slightly out, and weight on the inside of the feet **(Figure 2.26)**. Catchers should extend their glove-side elbow outside their knees, getting into the routine of providing a good target **(Figure 2.27)**. This position allows the catcher to receive the ball with a relaxed arm and wrist held in front of the body. It is critical that catchers protect their throwing hand from being hit by placing that hand behind their ankle **(Figure 2.28)**.

Blocking a Pitch

Catchers should react to a baseball thrown in the dirt by a coach or machine by dropping to their knees and tucking their chin into their chest protector.

They should quickly fill the 5-hole (the space created between the legs when the catcher falls to his or her knees) with an open glove while placing the bare hand behind the glove to protect it from being hit by the baseball. Catchers should lean slightly forward to block the baseball with their chest protector, and force the ball down to ground where they can get to their feet and pick it up **(Figure 2.29)**. Base runners at this level typically cannot advance on balls pitched in the dirt like they can at higher levels.

FIGURE 2.28

Catchers should protect their throwing hand by hiding it behind their ankle.

FIGURE 2.29

Teach catchers how to create a basic blocking position.

Work through the following drills and practice ideas to reinforce good catcher mechanics.

Specific Catcher Drills

 Refer to Coach-/Machine-Pitch (Ages 7–8) "Catcher Drills" on the DVD for the following drills:

A. Receiving tennis balls—Improves the mechanics and confidence of catching a baseball behind the plate with control.
B. Blocking tennis balls—Improves the mechanics and confidence of blocking a baseball behind the plate.

Additional Catcher Practice

A. Place a stationary ball on the ground behind home plate. Instruct the catcher, in full gear, to drop to a blocking position every time you point to the ball on the ground. Once in a while, you can throw a simulated pitch so that the catcher can receive the ball in the air, instead of blocking it. The catcher should quickly attempt to recover into a good receiving stance before responding to the next non-verbal command. Do three to five repetitions.

B. Instruct the catcher to put on his or her gear and create a good receiving stance. Simply throw soft baseballs to simulate a pitch. The player should catch the ball in the air on a good pitch and drop to a blocking position when the ball is going to hit the ground before being caught.

C. Let catchers put on their gear and get behind the plate during batting practice to get accustomed to catching and blocking the ball when a batter swings and misses or takes (does not swing at) a pitch. This will give them experience throwing the ball back to the mound.

FUNDAMENTAL OFFENSE SKILLS FOR COACH-PITCH / MACHINE-PITCH

The offensive focus for coach-pitch/machine-pitch baseball is on learning the correct swing mechanics to effectively hit a moving pitch. There are elements of simple baserunning for this age group, but they will be listed in the last section of this chapter. Seven- and eight-year-old players will no longer have the luxury of hitting a stationary ball off a batting tee. They will now have to develop the ability to track a moving baseball from a coach or machine, and use decision-making skills to determine if and when they will attempt a swing. They must learn how to overcome the inherent fear of being hit by a wild pitch.

Coaches and parents must recognize that there are simple elements of hitting that can significantly increase success or failure rates even before a player attempts to swing at a pitched ball. The bat the player chooses, where the player stands in the batter's box, how he or she grips the bat, and the player's basic stance are all critical elements to boost a player's success and ultimately build the confidence necessary to be a good hitter. The goal of every coach or parent should be to create simple pre-swing routines and establish fundamental swing mechanics.

When trying to eliminate swing flaws, never overwhelm hitters by giving them too much to think about at one time. This will lead to "paralysis by analysis" or the inability to do anything because they are trying to do too much. Simply begin by checking their distance from the plate, teaching a proper hitting stance, and reinforcing a correct grip of the bat. Once they have mastered those fundamentals, you can now move on to other issues impacting their success rate. It is important to help your players establish pre-pitch hitting routines where they do the same thing every time when they step into the batter's box; this prepares them mentally and physically to hit. Routines provide a level of comfort and help reduce the thinking process. An appropriate routine at this level includes checking themselves for a proper grip, stepping into the batter's box with the back foot first, and then bringing the front foot into place to square themselves up to the plate. Players should reach with the end of their bat to the far corner of the plate and then take a few practice swings. They should finish their routine by setting up their batting stance, ready to see the pitch. Teach players how to create some simple rhythm in their stance, such as moving their body a few inches back and forth in slow motion. This will help the hitter's muscles stay relaxed. It is always easier for batters to start their swing if the body is in motion instead of a more static position.

 Refer to Coach-/Machine-Pitch (Ages 7–8) "Hitting Mechanics" on the DVD for detailed interactive instruction.

The following is the minimum skill expectation for seven- and eight-year old players to swing a bat.

Proper Grip

Teach your players how to grip the bat by lining up the knuckles of the four fingers of each hand (minus the thumbs). It is very important for hitters to hold the bat where their fingers intersect with their palms because this is where they are strongest and will have the most control of the bat when they swing **(Figure 2.30)**.

FIGURE 2.30

Check hitters for a proper grip of the bat, making sure the "door-knocking" knuckles are close to being lined up.

FIGURE 2.31

Teach your hitters how to establish good plate coverage as a part of their setup in the batter's box.

FIGURE 2.32

Teach your hitter to create an athletic stance.

Good Plate Coverage

Teach your hitters to check themselves for good plate coverage. This helps ensure that batters are not too close nor far away from the plate. On a good swing, the goal is to be able to hit a pitch thrown over the plate with the barrel of the bat (Figure 2.31).

Correct Stance

Teach your players to achieve an athletic stance with feet placed slightly wider apart than shoulder width, knees and hips slightly flexed, and weight slightly forward with the head aligned just over the toes (Figure 2.32). The player's head should be straight up and down with both eyes focused on the coach or machine. The batter should raise his or her hands to a position approximately six inches off the back shoulder. Both elbows should relax and hang down. The angle of the bat should not be extreme, for instance, not pointed straight up, parallel to the ground, or wrapped around behind the hitter's head.

Simple Load and Stride

Teach your players how to move from their stance to a position that allows them to attack the ball. As the ball is about to be released by the coach

FIGURE 2.33

Teach hitters how to implement a stride and load to create a strong position to attack the pitch.

or machine, they should lift their front foot and take a short stride forward towards the pitcher. Simultaneously or just before the stride, hitters should move their hands a few inches to a position just over their back foot. This puts the body in a balanced and strong position to swing the bat. Some young hitters stride and load naturally, some will adjust once they are taught, and others will not be ready to address this phase of preparing to swing the bat **(Figure 2.33)**.

Contact

Teach your hitters the concept of letting the ball travel through space from the coach or machine to the plate before they swing the bat. Once the baseball approaches the hitting zone (the area around home plate where the barrel of the bat has a chance to hit the ball with a good swing), the batter should attack the baseball with an aggressive swing. The goal of the hitter is to keep his or her head and eyes still, and not jump at the ball, rise up on the toes, or lower the body to hit. The player's back heel (the one closest to the catcher) should start to rise off the ground to allow the hips to rotate through the swing naturally. The hitter's front leg should become firm, almost straight, as the bat connects with the baseball. Simultaneously on contact, the palm of the top hand should be pointed towards the sky and the palm of the bottom hand should point towards the ground **(Figure 2.34)**.

Extension

Teach your hitters what it means to "get extension through the ball." This gives hitters a greater margin for error in the timing of the swing and yet allows them to still hit the ball hard. The goal is to attack the baseball with a quick swing and then create good extension through the ball while finishing the swing. As the hitter gets extension through the ball with the bat, the back heel should continue to rotate heel to sky. The back heel

FIGURE 2.34

This hitter is making contact with the baseball with hands in a palm up/palm down position.

FIGURE 2.35

Teach the hitter to get full extension with the barrel of the bat to increase the chance of making solid contact.

should remain in this position through the completion of the swing **(Figure 2.35)**.

Finish

Teach hitters how to finish their swing with balance. Their head should be centered above the middle of the feet, and eyes should be focused on the contact point with the ball. Their hands should finish the swing near the front shoulder, with the bat behind them **(Figure 2.36)**. It is best to keep both hands on the bat (instead of releasing the bat with the top hand). If the player makes contact with the ball, he or she should run hard to first base.

FIGURE 2.36

Hitters should finish their swing in a balanced stance, with hands high and the back heel lifted towards the sky.

Work through the following drills and practice ideas to reinforce good swing mechanics.

Specific Hitting Drills

 Refer to Coach-/Machine-Pitch (Ages 7–8) "Hitting Drills"" on the DVD for the following drills:

A. Basic tee—Improves the fundamental swing mechanics of a hitter.
B. Double tee—Creates a good swing plane or bat path to the baseball with an emphasis on extension.
C. High tee—Helps hitters to create a correct swing path to the baseball.
D. Basketball tee—Helps hitters to create good extension through the ball.
E. Noodle tee—Helps hitters to create a short swing path to the ball.
F. Front foot platform—Prevents hitters from lunging or jumping at the ball.

Additional Hitting Practice

A. Side toss—Coaches can set up stations where they kneel off to the side of a hitter at a 45-degree angle. They can toss the ball underhand to the batter, who hits the ball into a net. If it is a bad feed, the hitter should not swing but wait for a good feed.
B. Front toss—Coaches can set up a protective screen such as an "L-screen" directly in front of, and a short distance away from, the hitter to ensure accuracy. The coach can feed a firm underhand toss to the hitter from the side of the screen (making sure to keep the hand and body behind the screen to prevent getting hit with a batted ball). This gives the batter many strikes from a realistic angle. It is a great way to get many swings in a short time and to build confidence. It is also a great drill if there is restricted space (use restricted-flight balls such as a Wiffle ball).
C. Batting practice from coach and/or machine—Simply throw balls to hit or use a pitching machine to simulate game play.

COACHING COACH-PITCH/MACHINE-PITCH 101: TEACHING GAME SKILLS

In order for children to successfully play a coach-pitch/machine-pitch game, coaches must prepare them for basic situations that will arise when competing against another team. Below is a simple list of offensive and defensive skills and situations that should be mastered by the time a player graduates coach-pitch or machine-pitch. Use practice time and games to reinforce these skills.

Team Offense—The Basics

Teach your players the following:

1. How to hit and run the bases aggressively.
2. How to run through first base (this is the only base besides home where this is allowed).
3. How to execute a turn at first base on a ball hit to the outfield past the infielders.
4. When it is safe to advance to the next base on their own as opposed to when they are required by the rules of baseball to advance. At the coach-pitch/machine-pitch level, coaches should avoid the temptation in games to play "cat and mouse" with their base runners to cause chaos for the defense. This eats up valuable game time and takes away from the opportunity to learn basic skills that must be mastered by players to move to higher levels of the game.
5. How and when to tag-up at third base on a fly ball.
6. How to slide feet-first into bases.
7. How to return to their original base on a ball caught in the air with fewer than two outs.
8. How to run the bases for a double, triple, and home run.

Coaches must keep order, organization, and safety in the dugout. This is a great job to assign to a "team mom" or "team dad" so the coaches can concentrate on teaching the game.

Team Defense—The Basics

Teach your players the following:

1. How to execute force outs at all bases in a forced situation.

2. How to recognize when base runners must be tagged out.

3. To always keep in mind, between pitches, how many outs there are and where they should throw the ball if it is hit to them in the air or on the ground.

4. When making plays from the outfield to the infield, where to throw the ball to keep base runners from advancing.

5. How to correctly communicate with their teammates when catching a fly ball.

6. How to stop the play (create a "dead ball"). Each league has different rules for ending a play at this level.

7. How to avoid falling into a trap from an offensive team that will intentionally play "cat and mouse" with their base runners to cause problems for the defense just to score runs.

POST-GAME TALK

At the conclusion of each game, the head coach should bring the team together into a group in the outfield or just outside the field of play. This should be done without the parents of the players, who can distract the children. The coach should review some of the simple things that were learned from that game.

- Ask players to take a knee (kneel) and face the coaches, giving the coaches their full attention.
- Each coach on staff should share one or two quick points about the game that can help the team improve.
- Coaches should focus on the positive aspects of the game as much as possible.
- Never single out a player for his or her mistakes. However, it is okay to use players as positive examples. Find good things to say about all your players, primarily focusing on a strong team concept.
- Never blame losses on the umpires or any other external factor such as the field playing conditions, weather, and so on.

- Remind players of the next practice or game, even though most players will not remember. This is teaching responsibility and players will need this skill as they grow older.
- Bring the team together for a simultaneous dismissal where all players put their hands together and shout "Team!"

The coach should have arranged in advance for parents to bring a team snack and drink to provide after each post-game talk.

Refer to Chapter 8, "Coaching Youth Baseball," for more ideas about how to conduct a productive and enjoyable baseball practice.

CHAPTER 3

MINIMUM SKILL EXPECTATION FOR PLAYER-PITCH BASEBALL (Ages 9–10)

Myth #1: BY THE AGE OF NINE OR TEN, PLAYERS SHOULD START SPECIALIZING IN ONE SPORT. THE MORE BASEBALL GAMES THAT PLAYERS CAN BE INVOLVED IN, THE BETTER THEY WILL BECOME.

Secret: Players should be involved in a solid baseball schedule in the spring and part of the summer, but they should not be expected to give up their childhood to play non-stop baseball. Beware! As they grow older, children who play too much baseball too soon typically lose their desire to compete. They also can suffer from overuse injuries (damage to critical joints, muscles, tendons, and ligaments) and become prone to arm problems at younger ages.

Myth #2: NOW THAT PLAYERS ARE PITCHING, IT IS IMPORTANT FOR THEM TO THROW A CURVEBALL SO THEY WILL BE SELECTED FOR THE ALL-STAR TEAM.

Secret: Curveballs should be avoided completely at this age because improper technique can cause injuries. Young players should focus on learning to throw fastballs and changeups for strikes. These two pitches can give pitchers longevity in the game without relying on a breaking pitch to deceive hitters.

Myth #3: AS WITH T-BALL AND COACH-PITCH/MACHINE-PITCH LEVELS, WINNING DOES NOT MATTER AT THE PLAYER-PITCH LEVEL.

Secret: At this age, winning does begin to matter to the kids, though it should not become the only focus of the games and practices. The participants know there are winners and losers, and they prefer to be on the winning side. However, they typically recover quickly from losses. This is the age when many players start to show their emotions, and they should be taught how to win or lose with sportsmanship and integrity.

Player-pitch baseball is typically the third tier of organized youth baseball. It provides exciting new opportunities for coaches and parents to reinforce fundamentals taught at earlier ages, while introducing appropriate skills and drills needed to succeed at this level and beyond. Players are increasingly defining "fun" in baseball as "winning." Therefore, adults must set an example by maintaining perspective on wins and losses while placing the appropriate emphasis on teaching participants how to play the game correctly.

By the ages of nine and ten, many players are beginning to perform fundamental skills without conscious thought. Similar to a computer, a player's brain and nervous system are gradually being programmed to perform the complex multi-joint movements needed to play the game successfully. Muscle memory is progressively embedded in the subconscious every time a player throws or fields a ball, makes a catch, or swings a bat. In baseball, we call these accumulated skills good habits or bad habits. Therefore, coaches and parents of players at this level should place a greater emphasis on fundamental skills being performed correctly from start to finish. They can do this by teaching more detail of each movement and through a variety of specific defensive and offensive drills. Players should be given adequate repetitions with all drills in order to reinforce correct skill movements and increase confidence. Quality of repetition is much more important than quantity of repetition.

The most significant offensive advancement in player-pitch baseball is that, for the first time, batters will be pitched to by children their own age. Hitters must learn to overcome the fear of being struck by a wild pitch. They must also refine their pitch recognition skills to adjust to the different types of pitches they may see. The most significant defensive advancement is that players become the "battery" (pitcher and catcher). Therefore, coaches and parents have the dual challenge of developing and refining the key skill of hitting while simultaneously developing pitchers who can consistently throw strikes as well as catchers who can receive the pitches.

It is critical that coaches run practices that are fun, efficient, challenging, high-energy, and positive. This will help to keep players interested in playing baseball despite the slow pace of actual games. Parents must also stay positive and help their child work on individual weaknesses. The more players on a team who possess the fundamental skills of throwing, catching, fielding, baserunning, and hitting, the cleaner and faster-paced the games will be played. Coaches should have detailed knowledge of the above skills and corresponding drills, along with a few specific plays used to score runs or to prevent runs from being scored.

Some players at this level are ready for more advanced skills, especially with season-ending all-star teams that are composed of more proficient players. However, rushing all players in this age group into more advanced skills can be detrimental to their progress and even cause them to physically or mentally take steps backwards. It is vital to keep the player's ability level in perspective. Coaches and parents should never find themselves making it a job for their kids to play baseball. Too much pressure from adults can steal the joy from the game.

FUNDAMENTAL DEFENSE SKILLS FOR PLAYER-PITCH BASEBALL

Coaches and parents should continue to place a significant emphasis on refining the fundamental defensive skills of throwing, catching, fielding ground balls, fielding fly balls, pitching, and catcher play. These are the basic skills that will be needed to play the game successfully at higher levels. Players should continue to be exposed to a variety of defensive positions. It is much too early in player development to specialize. What may seem like an ideal defensive position for a player at this age may change when his or her body goes through puberty. The more experience a player has at other positions, the more valuable he or she will be to future teams as they grow older, and this can increase their playing time.

Baseball is the only team sport in which the defense is in control of the ball. Even though players are more skilled and physically stronger than in the previous two beginning levels of baseball, typically the speed of games remains very slow. This is due to the inability of pitchers to throw consistent strikes, and most catchers struggle to receive pitches cleanly. Catchers often wear out a path to the backstop to retrieve the ball and throw it back to the pitcher. As a result, teams will typically score more runs from batters walking, stealing bases (if allowed in your league), or advancing on passed balls than from stringing together hits.

THROWING MECHANICS

By ages nine and ten, most players are more comfortable with the sister skills of throwing and catching the ball. Therefore, coaches and parents should pay greater attention to the fine details of throwing mechanics. Players should always throw to a specific target such as a player's chest, rather than a general destination such as another person. Systematically make adjustments to reduce flaws and improve accuracy. When throwing a baseball, the body parts link together to form a kinetic chain. Each body part transfers energy to another until it is eventually released into the baseball as it is propelled away from the body. Throwing accuracy has much to do with players correctly positioning their feet, aligning their upper body, and creating good direction towards the target.

 Refer to Player-Pitch (Ages 9–10) "Throwing Mechanics" on the DVD for detailed interactive instruction.

The following phases are the minimum skill progression needed for a player-pitch player to throw a ball.

Proper Grip

Teach players to hold the baseball away from the palm of the hand with a two-finger, four-seam throwing grip. All throwers should place the pads of their pointer and middle fingers on top seams of the ball and the thumb under the center of the ball, splitting the distance between the top two fingers. The ring finger and pinkie rest on the side of the ball to help balance it in the hand. Pitchers can also implement appropriate alternate grips such as a two-seam grip or changeup grip **(Figure 3.1)**.

Momentum and Alignment

Teach players to take an initial step with their throwing-side foot, turning it perpendicular towards the target. This action helps gain momentum and puts the body into a good throwing position. Next, they should simultaneously turn the front shoulder to point at the target while striding in opposition with the glove-side foot; i.e., right-handed throwers step with their left foot **(Figure 3.2)**.

FIGURE 3.1

Defensive players should hold the baseball across the horseshoe of the laces with a four-seam grip.

FIGURE 3.2

Players should take an inward step with the throwing-side foot to simultaneously gain momentum and align with the target.

Power Position

The player's eyes should be focused on the target. The front or glove-side elbow should be approximately shoulder-high and pointed directly at the target. The throwing elbow should also be approximately shoulder-high, creating a backwards "L", and it should be pointed away from the target. The ball should be gripped correctly, with the wrist relaxed, pointed outward, and away from the target. The bottom half of the body should be in a good athletic position with the player's feet placed wider than his or her shoulders, knees slightly bent, and hips slightly flexed **(Figure 3.3)**.

Throwing the Ball

The player should accelerate the baseball from behind his or her body to a point out in front of the body where it is released towards the target, while simultaneously keeping the chin directly pointed at the target. The two primary throwing fingers should stay on top and behind the ball, and the throwing elbow should remain shoulder-high through release. As the player's momentum continues forward through the throw, the throwing-arm elbow and the glove-arm elbow get closer to each other. This reduces

FIGURE 3.3

Players should initiate a good power position in order to make accurate throws.

FIGURE 3.4

This player demonstrates proper body alignment and glove position for good direction to the target.

the player's chance of working across the body, which would result in an inconsistent release point. The bottom half of the player's body simultaneously puts energy into the throw by pushing off the ground with the back leg to rotate the hips **(Figure 3.4)**. Players should simulate throwing down a narrow hallway, taking care not to bump into the imaginary walls with body parts or the ball.

Extension to Target

The player must extend his or her throwing arm completely towards the target and snap the wrist to let go of the ball creating a backwards, or twelve-o'clock to six-o'clock, rotation. The top two fingers of the throwing hand should stay behind and on top of the baseball through release. The player's head should continue to move towards the target and align with his or her front knee when the ball leaves the hand. Simultaneously, the glove-arm elbow moves behind the glove-side hip to allow for a good finish to the throw **(Figure 3.5)**.

Follow Through

Once the player releases the ball, he or she should complete the throwing process by allowing the arm to decelerate naturally and finish just outside

FIGURE 3.5

To increase accuracy, players should extend the throwing arm towards the target on release.

FIGURE 3.6

To increase accuracy and reduce the risk of injury, throwers should learn to follow through completely.

the stride-foot knee. The back foot will simultaneously release off the ground, heel to the sky, and eventually finish forward near or past the stride foot. This allows the hips to finish rotating and for momentum to continue forward towards the target. The player's head should finish in front of his or her front knee while the glove-arm elbow should end up behind the hip, allowing the shoulders to finish naturally **(Figure 3.6)**.

Work through the following drills and practice ideas to reinforce good throwing mechanics.

Specific Throwing Drills

 Refer to Player-Pitch (Ages 9–10) "Throwing Drills" on the DVD for the following drills:

- Kneeling figure eight—Reinforces rhythm and tempo in the upper body when throwing the ball.
- Kneeling power position—Reinforces a good power position before the throw to improve accuracy.
- Standing figure eight—Creates rhythm and tempo with the whole body when throwing the ball.

- Standing power position—Creates a correct power position with the lower and upper body when throwing the ball.
- Boxers—Creates rhythm and teaches how to transfer energy from the back side of the body to the front side.
- Jumpbacks—Teaches players how to incorporate their whole body when throwing the ball.
- Throwing long—Increases arm strength.

Additional Throwing Practice

A. 21 Points—This game should only be played with players who are proficient at catching the ball so no one gets hurt. Teach players to assign points to upper body parts, such as five points for the head and two points for the center of the chest. Pair up players; all groups of two must be equal distance away from one another, 25 to 35 feet is recommended. Instruct players that they are not permitted to aim the ball or move out of the way to prevent points. Players take turns making firm, accurate throws that are caught by their partner. If the caught ball was on target to the head, the thrower gets 5 points towards reaching the total of 21. If the caught throw would have made contact in between the shoulders, 2 points are awarded. If only two players are competing, the first to reach or pass 21 wins. If groups of two players are competing as a team, the first team to total a combined 21 points or above is the winner.

B. Relay game—Divide your team into equal groups and place players in a straight line 20 to 30 feet apart from one another. Create two to four parallel lines across the field. Give the first player in each line a ball. On the coach's command, the players start throwing down their line as quickly as possible. If they overthrow their partner or their partner misses the ball, it must go back to the thrower and they try that exchange again. Keys include throwing to their partner's glove side, receivers using two hands to catch, and then turning to their glove side to throw to the next partner in line. The last player in line catches the ball and starts it to the front of the line using the same pattern. Players are never allowed to skip people in their line. The ball must be caught and thrown, one player at a time, as it moves from front to back or back to front. The coach determines how many times the ball must successfully make its way up and down before a winner is crowned. The losing teams usually pay consequences, such as executing five push-ups. Competing makes players concentrate more.

C. Four-seam grip practice—Players spend time at home softly tossing the ball up and catching it, or spinning it and catching it. They must reach into the glove and quickly feel for a four-seam grip across the horseshoe of the laces. Players must learn to rotate the ball in their throwing hand, fingers in an "up and to the right" rotation until they come to the four-seam grip. Players should avoid looking at the ball; this process is done by feel and not sight.

CATCHING THROWN BASEBALLS

This is the final age group in which the skill of receiving or catching a baseball will be discussed separately from addressing specific defensive positions. At the player-pitch level, participants should become more proficient at catching thrown baseballs. This includes baseballs thrown directly at them, to their side, and off-line in all directions. Players should be taught the concept of moving their feet to catch every thrown ball in the center of their body (between their shoulders). This puts the receiver in a good position to make a quick transition from the glove to the throwing hand. Teach players to control the baseball or "dominate" the ball when it enters the glove so the force of the ball does not snap the glove backwards. To accomplish this, players must keep their glove wrist relaxed and glove-arm elbow flexed (but firm) when the ball is caught. The ball should make a popping sound in the glove, as it impacts the pocket for a catch. As players advance to higher levels, they will learn that in certain circumstances the ball is not always caught, but rather it is stopped by the glove and redirected into the hand for the quickest transition possible.

 Refer to Player-Pitch (Ages 9–10) "Catching the Ball" on the DVD for detailed interactive instruction.

The following is the minimal skill progression needed for nine- and ten-year-old players to catch a thrown ball.

Above-the-Belt Catches

Teach players to make various catches above the belt line with their glove fingers up (towards the sky). This includes balls thrown at them, to their glove side, or to their backhand side. Players should become confident catching baseballs thrown to them above the belt at various speeds without intentionally moving out of the way to catch the ball on either side of their body **(Figures 3.7, 3.8, 3.9)**.

FIGURE 3.7

When catching a baseball above the belt, players should try to receive the ball between the shoulders with fingers towards the sky.

FIGURE 3.8

When players cannot get in front of the ball to catch it above the belt, one option is to receive it on the glove side of the body, fingers up.

FIGURE 3.9

Players also have the option to receive the ball, fingers up, on the backhand side of the body, when they can't get in front of the ball to catch it above the belt.

Below-the-Belt Catches

Teach players to catch balls below the belt line with their glove fingers down (towards the ground). This includes throws directly at them, to their glove side, or to their backhand side. The most difficult catch is typically the backhand catch below the belt line. Players should become confident catching baseballs thrown to them below the belt at various speeds without intentionally moving out of the way to catch the ball on either side of their body **(Figures 3.10, 3.11)**.

fingertips of the glove should touch the ground at the top of an imaginary triangle created by the top of both feet and the mitt. The glove should be open to receive the baseball and then closed once the ball enters. The throwing hand should be above the glove, ready to secure the ball in the glove and quickly take it out to throw it. The player's head and eyes should follow the moving baseball into the glove for a catch. The goal is to catch the ball in front of the body, which will help the fielder quickly transition into a power position **(Figure 3.14)**.

Power Position

Teach players how to efficiently link energy from their fielding triangle position to their power position by quickly taking the ball out of their glove and moving their feet to turn their body perpendicular or sideways to their target. This process provides momentum towards the intended base, without needing to take extra steps, which makes it easier to consistently throw base runners out at first base. Once the fielder is in a power position, the ball should be behind the body, pointed away from the target with a relaxed grip. The back elbow is approximately shoulder-high. The front shoulder, elbow, hip, and toe should all end up pointed at the target. The player is now ready to throw the ball **(Figure 3.15)**.

FIGURE 3.14

Instruct players on how to create a good fielding position in order to consistently catch the baseball.

FIGURE 3.15

Teach players how to move their feet and body from their fielding position into their power position.

Throw and Extension

This phase happens very quickly to the naked eye. The player should accelerate the baseball from behind his or her body to a point out in front of the body, where it is released towards the target. The two primary throwing fingers should stay on top and behind the ball, and the throwing elbow should remain shoulder-high through release. As the player's momentum continues forward through the throw, the glove-arm elbow and the throwing-arm elbow move closer together. This action reduces the player's chance of working across the body, which would result in an inconsistent release point. The bottom half of the fielder's body simultaneously adds energy into the throw by driving off the ground with the back leg, accelerating the hips into rotation. Upon releasing the ball, the fielder should extend his or her throwing arm completely towards the target and snap their wrist, creating backwards (or twelve-o'clock to six-o'clock) rotation (**Figures 3.16, 3.17**).

Follow Through

Once the player releases the ball towards the target, he or she should complete the throw by allowing their arm to decelerate naturally and

FIGURE 3.16

The fielder begins the throw to first base by keeping the throwing elbow shoulder-high.

FIGURE 3.17

The fielder gets good extension to first base while maintaining good direction with his glove side.

finish just outside their stride-foot knee. The back foot will simultaneously release off the ground, heel to the sky, and eventually finish forward, near or past the stride foot. This allows the hips to finish rotating and for momentum to continue forward. The player's head should finish in front of the front knee while the glove-arm elbow should end up behind the hip, allowing the shoulders to finish naturally. Once the ball is gone, the fielder should maintain momentum for a few steps towards first base **(Figure 3.18)**.

FIGURE 3.18

Teach the infielder to properly finish the throw and maintain momentum.

Work through the following fielding drills and practice ideas to reinforce good fielding mechanics.

Specific Fielding Drills

 Refer to Player-Pitch (Ages 9–10) "Infield Drills" on the DVD for the following drills:

A. Fielding mechanics—Improves fielding mechanics by breaking down the process into specific phases and building it back up to a complete skill.
B. Short hops—Improves a fielder's ability to handle short hops at them to the backhand and the glove side.
C. Three-step/five-step—Improves a player's first step to a ground ball and the ability to move into a good fielding position.
D. Fly ball drill—Improves a fielder's ability to handle fly balls around the infield. This addresses the tendency of many to work on ground balls and fielding drills while neglecting infield fly balls.

Additional Fielding Practice

A. Fielding triangle throws—While you are implementing the throwing mechanics taught earlier in the chapter, infielders can spend time getting into a perfect fielding position with the ball in their glove prior to making a throw. The fielder then moves his or her body into a power position and finishes with a quick throw to their partner or adult.

B. Shadow fielding—Players mimic the actions of a coach or parent to creep into a good ready position, fielding position, power position, and then make the throw or act like they're making a throw.

C. Wall ball—Players can throw a tennis ball into a wall and move their body to field the ball in a perfect fielding position.

D. Live repetitions—First, roll groundballs to the player, then hit them to the player, and eventually progress to game-like repetitions, where a player fields and throws to a base. This is necessary for infielders to develop consistency and confidence to perform in the game.

E. Jumping rope—Jumping rope is a great strategy to improve footwork. Players need quick feet to be consistent fielders.

DOUBLE PLAY FEEDS AND PIVOTS

A double play is a defensive maneuver that infielders should learn and begin to use at this age level. When middle infielders (shortstop and second basemen) complete a double play, it usually consists of both a feed and a pivot executed by the shortstop and the second baseman to record two force outs on one batted ground ball. When there are runners on first base or first and second bases, and less than two outs, the middle infielders should move a few steps closer to second base to create double-play depth. In this position, they can get to second base with enough time to execute the play. A 6-4-3 double play consists of a feed made by the shortstop (6), a pivot executed by the second baseman (4), and a catch of a thrown ball by the first baseman (3). A 4-6-3 double play consists of a feed made by the second baseman (4), a pivot executed by the shortstop (6), and a catch of a thrown ball by the first baseman (3). As players grow in strength, skill, and experience in years to come, the types of double play feeds and pivots used by infielders will become more complex. Commonly, third basemen, shortstops, and second basemen are right-handed throwers. First basemen can throw with either right or left hands.

Refer to Player-Pitch (Ages 9–10) "Double Play Feeds and Pivots" on the DVD for detailed interactive instruction.

The following is the minimal skill progression needed for nine- and ten-year-old players to execute the most basic double play feeds and pivots in the middle infield.

Shortstop Flip: Feed

This is a basic double play feed made by a shortstop to a second baseman when the ground ball is hit at or to the left of the shortstop. Because the momentum of the play takes the shortstop towards second base, he or she should make the feeds underhand.

Teach the shortstop to charge the ground ball, if there is time, and get into a good fielding position. This creates momentum that will be used to make the flip feed. The fielder should shout "flip, flip, flip" to let the second baseman know the ball will be delivered underhand **(Figure 3.19)**.

Separation

Teach the shortstop how to correctly field the ball with both hands working together to quickly separate the ball from the glove. Once the ball is in the fielder's bare hand, he or she should create space between the glove and the ball so the second baseman can easily see the feed **(Figure 3.20)**.

FIGURE 3.19

Shortstops should cut down the distance to the ball and get into a good fielding position to start an underhand flip feed.

FIGURE 3.20

The shortstop should quickly separate the ball from the glove to be in a position to make the flip feed to the second baseman.

FIGURE 3.21

The shortstop's legs should generate momentum to feed the ball to
the second baseman.

FIGURE 3.22

After the feed is made, the shortstop should continue moving to a
point past second base.

Delivery

To avoid wasting valuable time, the shortstop should stay low to the
ground, gradually raising his or her body through the phases of the flip
feed. The fielder's wrist (with the ball) should lock, in order to decrease the
ball's rotation as he or she simultaneously pulls the glove into their chest
to expose the ball to the second baseman. The fielder should use his or her
leg strength to continue momentum towards second base **(Figure 3.21)**,
and release a firm feed in the direction of the front corner of the base (the
corner closest to the pitcher's mound). A good flip feed should be received
by the second baseman somewhere from belt- to chest-height.

Follow

Once the feed has been released to the second baseman, the shortstop
should maintain his or her momentum by continuing past second base
(Figure 3.22).

Second Baseman Left Foot On/Off: Pivot

This is a basic double play pivot made when the ball is hit to the left side
of the infield (to the shortstop or third baseman). The second baseman
should hustle to second base to be ready for a possible double play feed. As

the fielder approaches the base, he or she should widen their legs to get under control. The right foot should be positioned on the clay next to the back corner of the base (the corner closest to center field) and the left foot should be on the base. The second baseman's body should be squared to the shortstop (or third baseman if they are making the feed) with knees and hips flexed in a good athletic position. The second baseman's glove should be open, with the throwing hand close by, as if his or her thumbs were tied together with a short string, giving the fielder a good target to feed the ball **(Figure 3.23)**.

FIGURE **3.23**

The second baseman should quickly move to the bag and get into position, with the left foot on the base and the shoulders squared to the fielder making the feed.

Power Position and Throw

Once the second baseman receives the feed, he or she simply removes their left foot from the base, plants it on the clay to create a good power position, and uses good throwing mechanics to release the ball to first base. He or she should avoid taking extra steps to make their throw **(Figure 3.24)**.

Second Baseman Flip: Feed

This is a basic double play feed made by a second baseman to a shortstop when a ground ball is hit at the fielder or takes them towards second base. If there is time, the second baseman should charge the ground ball and get into a good fielding position. This creates momentum, which will be used to make the flip feed. The fielder should shout "flip, flip, flip" to the shortstop to let him or her know that the ball will be delivered in an underhand fashion **(Figure 3.25)**.

FIGURE **3.24**

Teach the second baseman to quickly remove his or her left foot from the base, create a power position, and throw to first base.

79

FIGURE 3.25

The second baseman should close the distance to the ball and get into a good fielding position to start an underhand flip feed.

FIGURE 3.26

The second baseman should quickly separate the ball from the glove to be in a position to make the flip feed to the shortstop.

Separation

Teach the second baseman how to correctly field the ball with both hands working together to quickly separate the ball from the glove. Once the ball is in the bare hand, the fielder should create space between the glove and ball in order for the shortstop to easily see the feed **(Figure 3.26)**.

Delivery

To avoid wasting valuable time, the second baseman should stay low to the ground, gradually raising his or her body through the phases of the flip feed. The fielder's wrist (with the ball) should lock, in order to decrease the ball's rotation as he or she simultaneously pulls their glove into their chest to expose the ball to the shortstop. The fielder should use his or her leg strength to continue momentum towards second base **(Figure 3.27)**, and release a firm feed in the direction of the back corner of the base (the corner closest to the right field). A good flip feed should be received by the shortstop somewhere from belt- to chest-height.

FIGURE 3.27

The second baseman's legs should generate momentum as he or she flips the ball underhanded to the shortstop to start a double play.

FIGURE 3.28

After the feed is made, the second baseman should continue moving to a point past second base.

Follow

Once the feed has been released to the shortstop, the second baseman should maintain his or her momentum by continuing past second base **(Figure 3.28)**.

Shortstop Turn: Pivot

This is a basic double play pivot made by the shortstop when the ball is hit to the right side of the infield (to the second baseman or first baseman). The fielder should quickly move to second base to be ready for a possible double play feed. As the shortstop approaches the base, he or she should raise their glove, widen their legs to gain body control, and square their shoulders to the feeder. The glove should be open, in front of player's body, and near the back corner of the base (the corner closest to the right fielder). This creates a good target for the second baseman. The shortstop's throwing hand should be very close to his or her glove, as if their thumbs were tied together with a short string, ready to make a quick transition to throw to first base **(Figure 3.29)**.

FIGURE 3.29

The shortstop should get to the base quickly, ready to receive the double play feed and to provide a good target for the second baseman.

FIGURE 3.30

The shortstop should simultaneously step to the feed with his or her left foot while receiving the ball in the glove, making sure to keep the throwing hand close to the glove.

Bag Swipe

When the shortstop recognizes the feed is on target, he or she should step to the ball with their left foot while reaching out to receive the ball with the glove, being careful not to lock their arms. Simultaneously, their right foot should drag or swipe across the back of the base to record the first out of the double play **(Figure 3.30)**.

Power Position

As the shortstop drags his or her right foot across the back of the base, he or she should use lower body strength to counteract inertia or momentum. This allows the player to redirect their body into a good power position and make a good throw to first base **(Figure 3.31)**.

FIGURE 3.31

The shortstop should use the right foot to swipe the back of second base and redirect their body into a good power position to first base.

Work through the following double play drills and practice ideas to reinforce good feed and pivot mechanics.

Specific Double Play Drills

A. Box feeds—Improves flip feed mechanics for shortstop and second basemen. The coach creates a square of middle infielders, placing portable bases 15 feet apart (create a triangle if there are only three players). The coach should focus individually on the flip feed of either the shortstop or the second baseman. The ball starts in the glove of one player, who creates a perfect fielding position at his or her base. When ready, the fielder makes a flip feed to the base to his or her left to simulate a shortstop flip feed, and then to the base to the right to simulate a second-baseman flip feed. When the partner at the base catches the ball, that player continues the pattern of the drill by getting into a fielding position and making the next flip feed. The process continues around the square until the coach stops it.

B. Box pivots—Improves the double play pivot mechanics for shortstop and second basemen. Like the previous drill, the coach creates a square of middle infielders, placing the portable bases 15 to 20 feet apart. The coach should focus individually on either the shortstop's pivot or the second baseman's pivot. All fielders should perform the same pivot for a few rotations before changing to the other pivot. One player starts with the ball in his or her glove at their base. The player to their left either positions his or her feet for a "left foot on—left foot off" pivot of a second baseman or a swipe pivot of a shortstop. The player with the ball throws it overhand to the player who executes the pivot and finishes with a simulated throw to first base. It is now that player's turn to start the drill again. He or she throws the ball to the player to the left, who executes the same pivot and simulates a throw to first base. The most recent player to execute the pivot becomes the next person to start the drill over, and the ball eventually makes its way around the square.

Additional Double Play Practice

A. Dry flip feeds—The coach or parent starts the shortstop or second baseman in a perfect fielding position with a ball in the player's glove. On command, the middle infielders use their legs to create momentum and execute a flip feed to second base.

B. Dry pivots—The coach or parent starts the shortstop or second baseman at double play depth with the ball in the player's glove. On command, the middle infielder quickly approaches second base to simulate receiving a feed. This allows the fielder to concentrate on the footwork of the pivot without worrying about receiving the actual feed. The player finishes the pivot by making a throw to first base.

C. Rolled flip feeds—The coach or parent should roll a simulated ground ball to the middle infielder (shortstop or second baseman), who can work on charging the ball and getting into a good fielding position before executing the mechanics of a flip feed.

D. Controlled pivots—The coach or parent starts the shortstop or second baseman in double play depth. On command, the middle infielder breaks to second base, ready to make the pivot. When the player nears the base, the adult makes a throw (simulated feed) for the shortstop or second baseman to execute a pivot. The fielder can finish the pivot by simulating a throw to first base, actually making a throw to a first baseman, or throwing to a screen at first base.

FIRST BASE MECHANICS

Due to improved skills, strength, and experience at the player-pitch level, infielders will begin to make more consistent force outs by fielding a ground ball and throwing out runners at first base. This accentuates the importance of the first baseman as a key defense component when it comes to developing a competitive team. It is critical that coaches spend practice time with children who may potentially play first base to educate them on vital skills including basic footwork around the base, stretching for the ball, picking up balls thrown in the dirt, and making tags on errant throws up the base line that take the fielder into the path of the base runner. A good first baseman makes everyone in the infield better if he or she has good footwork around the base and can make difficult catches.

The following is the minimum skill progression needed for a nine- or ten-year old to play the position of first base.

FIGURE 3.32

The first baseman should quickly get to the base, place both heels on the side of the base, and square his or her body to the person throwing the ball.

FIGURE 3.33

The first baseman should wait for the ball to get close to the base before stretching to receive an accurate throw.

Setup at First Base

Teach the first baseman to move quickly to the base when the ball is hit to the infield. The player should place both heels on the side of first base parallel to the foul line to create a safe distance from the base runner. He or she should square their body to face the person making the throw, remain relaxed, and be ready to stretch for a good throw or react to a bad throw (Figure 3.32).

Stretch for the Ball

The first baseman should wait and see whether the throw is on target before committing to stretch to catch the ball. When the thrown baseball is close to first base, the player must stride towards the ball with his or her glove-side foot and reach with the glove to meet and receive the baseball. The first baseman's throwing-side foot must stay on the side of the base for the force out. If the throw is off target, the first baseman should abandon the base to stop the ball from getting past him or her. After stopping the ball, he or she should attempt to tag the base runner if they have not yet reached first base (Figure 3.33).

FIGURE 3.34

Teach first basemen how to adjust their footwork to the outfield side in order to catch a ball thrown off-target.

FIGURE 3.35

First basemen can also adjust their footwork to the infield side to catch a ball thrown to the home plate side of the base.

Footwork on Poor Throws

When receiving throws off the baseline, first basemen should be taught how to adjust their feet on the base in order to increase their reach in the direction of the throw. To receive a throw to the right field side of the base, the first baseman should shift both heels to the far side (outfield side) of the base before stretching to catch the ball. To receive a throw to the home plate side of the base, the first baseman should shift both heels to the infield side of the base before stretching to catch the ball. It is critical that first basemen keep their throwing-side foot on the base to record a possible force out. If the throw requires the first baseman to vacate the base, he or she should come off the base, make the catch, and if there is time, attempt to tag the base runner. Whenever a first baseman tags a runner, he or she should spin with the person to disseminate some of the energy of a possible collision, decrease the odds of a potential injury, and reduce the chance of the ball coming out of the glove (**Figures 3.34, 3.35**).

Picking the Ball

Picking or digging an errant throw out of the dirt is the most difficult catch to teach first basemen. Some throws will bounce somewhere before the base. First basemen must be taught the fundamentals of how to execute a pick, and they must work related drills to gain the instincts and confidence to make the tough play. When first basemen determine that they cannot stretch to catch the ball in the air, they must bend their knees to lower their body and glove to the ground. Once the ball is close to the base, they should start the glove low to the clay and stretch to the ball, moving their glove through the hop. A short hop or a long hop is the best to field (**Figure 3.36**).

Work through the following drills and practice ideas to reinforce good first base mechanics.

FIGURE **3.36**

Teach first basemen how to catch or pick an errant throw out of the dirt by keeping their body and glove low, and moving the mitt through the hop.

Specific First Base Drills

A. Semicircle receiving and picks—Improves the confidence of a first baseman stretching to catch the ball in the air or in the dirt thrown from all infield positions. Two players (or more) and a coach get 20 feet away from first base (with a ball in their glove) forming a semicircle around the base. Each feeder should be in the general direction of an infield position (third base, shortstop, second base). All three feeders alternate throwing the ball to the first baseman, who implements correct footwork at the base and stretches to make the proper catch. The first baseman then throws the ball back to the person who made the feed. Begin with throws in the air and then progress to throws in the dirt. Finally, alternate the type of throw in order for the first baseman to react to different types of throws.

B. Errant throws and tag—Improves a first baseman's ability to catch an errant throw up the line towards the base runner, and to make a corresponding tag. A coach should instruct the first baseman to start at his or her defensive position. On command, the player should run to the base and quickly set up, facing the coach. The coach should then make an errant throw up the base line in the air or in the dirt. If the first baseman cannot stay on the base to make the catch, he or she should abandon the base, make the catch, and then reach back attempting to tag the imaginary base runner. Remind the fielder to spin with the runner to help avoid injury.

Additional First Base Practice

A. Hit ground balls to the infield and instruct players to make throws to first base to complete a force out. First basemen should start in their defensive position and quickly move to set up at first base and receive the throw.

B. Move around the infield using a small T-ball bat or small youth bat to hit one-handed balls to simulate throws to the first basemen. Be sure not to hit the ball too hard or make the plays too difficult—this drill has the potential to discourage first basemen if they experience too much failure or if they get hit with the ball. They must react to the ball with proper footwork around the base. They should stretch to catch it in the air, on the ground, and, when necessary, come off the base to make a catch. The coach or parent should have good bat control in order to implement this practice idea.

OUTFIELD MECHANICS

At the player-pitch level, outfield play becomes an increasingly significant aspect of the game. Catching a routine fly ball or ground ball has become developmentally appropriate due to improved hand-eye coordination, body control, and receiving ability; as a result children begin to have more success making plays. However, there will still be plenty of batted balls that will be missed due to the speed, trajectory, and distance of the ball from the fielder. Coaches should review and implement the fundamental outfield principles that players of this age should know: taking good angles on their approach to the ball, keeping their eyes focused on the ball, running soft on their feet, hustling to the play, moving through the catch, and implementing a quality crow hop. Fielders should also be introduced to drills that emphasize these key outfield skills. Practice time should be allotted to teach fundamental cut-off and relay situations. Provide outfielders with experience executing plays based on the number of outs, game score, the number of runners on base, and whether the ball is being caught in the air or on the ground. Rotating players as base runners will help the defense see the play develop and recognize the consequences of a misplayed ball, or throwing the ball to the wrong base.

Refer to Player-Pitch (Ages 9–10) "Outfield Mechanics" on the DVD for detailed interactive instruction.

The following is the minimum skill set needed for nine- and ten-year old players to catch fly balls and ground balls in the outfield.

Creep into Ready Position

Teach outfielders how to creep (take small steps towards the plate, one foot at a time) into a ready position before every pitch in order to be in a good position to react to a batted ball. Before the ball reaches the plate, the fielder takes a small step forward foot by foot. The player's body should end up in an athletic position with feet spread wider than the shoulders, knees slightly bent, hips slightly flexed, weight slightly forward, glove out in front of the body with the pocket facing the batter, and eyes on the hitter **(Figure 3.37)**.

FIGURE 3.37

Teach outfielders how to creep into a good ready position so they can quickly react to a batted ball.

Drop Step or Crossover Step

Through instruction, drill work, and experience, outfielders must develop the ability to judge where gravity will bring a fly ball back to earth. They must implement the skill of quickly moving their body to that spot to be in a position to make a catch. If the outfielders determine the fly ball will land behind them, they should take a drop step to create a good angle to approach the ball. A drop step is executed by opening the hips and taking a backwards step to open the body in a good direction to make a catch. If the ball is hit directly to the outfielder's side, or towards the infield, he or she should execute a crossover step. A crossover step is simply stepping across the body, such as right foot crossing in front of left, to gain the most ground possible in the shortest amount of steps to create a good angle of approach and quickly get to the ball **(Figures 3.38, 3.39)**.

FIGURE 3.38

Baseballs hit behind an outfielder require a drop step to take a good angle to the play.

FIGURE 3.39

Baseballs hit to the outfielders' sides or towards the infield require a crossover step to take a good angle to the play.

Travel to the Ball

It is critical that outfielders quickly get to the projected destination of a fly ball while keeping their eyes fixed on the white dot in the sky as they run. This allows them to make last-second adjustments to get into the best possible position for the catch. Teach players to run softly on their feet to prevent their head from jarring up and down, which creates the illusion of the ball bouncing in the sky. Outfielders should avoid running for a catch with their glove arm extended because this slows them down. They should lift and open the glove to the ball just before the catch to save valuable time **(Figure 3.40)**.

FIGURE 3.40

Teach outfielders to run softly on their feet as they quickly move to make the play.

Advanced: Move Through the Ball

Coaches should introduce outfielders to the concept of working through a fly ball before making the actual catch in order to gain momentum towards their throwing target. If the fly ball is easy for the outfielder to handle, he or she should quickly move to a spot a short distance behind where the ball will intersect the ground. Once the player arrives at that spot, he or she should immediately redirect their momentum by squaring their shoulders towards their throwing target. When the ball is nearing the ground, the outfielder should move forward through the ball to make the catch **(Figure 3.41)**.

FIGURE **3.41**

The outfielder should move behind where the ball will land to gain momentum to make the throw.

Make the Catch

For a routine play, teach outfielders to position their throwing-side foot behind them, ready to accelerate their body in the direction of their throw, once the ball is secured. Players should make the catch above their face, letting the ball travel to their glove (they should avoid stabbing at it or jumping to it). They should firmly secure the catch by placing their bare hand on top of the ball. This allows for a quick transition into the throwing hand **(Figure 3.42)**.

FIGURE **3.42**

Outfielders should attempt to catch the ball in front of their face, track it into the glove, and make an efficient transition to throw.

Crow Hop

Outfielders should learn how to implement a crow hop, which makes it easier to throw the ball with more velocity and distance. As the ball is caught, the fielder should simultaneously drive his or her back leg forward towards the target. This creates additional momentum to throw the ball while turning the body into a power position without wasting valuable time. The focus should be on driving forward and not jumping up **(Figure 3.43)**.

Power Position

In the power position, the hand holding the ball should be behind the outfielder's body, pointed away from the target with a relaxed grip. The back elbow is approximately shoulder-high. The front shoulder, elbow, hip, and toe all should be pointed at the target **(Figure 3.44)**.

Throw and Extension

The two phases of throwing and extension combine to make one complete movement. These happen very quickly to the naked eye. The outfielder should accelerate the baseball from behind his or her body to the release point out in front of the body while maintaining momentum towards the target. The bottom half of the fielder's body simultaneously thrusts energy into the throw by pushing off the grass with the back leg, accelerating the

FIGURE 3.43

Outfielders should drive their throwing-side foot forward towards the target to execute a crow hop.

FIGURE 3.44

Outfielders should move their body into a good power position to make an accurate throw to their target.

FIGURE 3.45

Outfielders should begin the throw by keeping the throwing elbow shoulder-high.

FIGURE 3.46

To improve throwing accuracy, teach outfielders to achieve good extension while maintaining good direction with their glove side.

hips into rotation. The fielder should extend the throwing hand completely towards the target to release the ball, snapping the wrist hard to create backwards, or twelve-o'clock to six-o'clock, rotation. The thrower's head should be aligned directly above the front knee when the ball leaves the hand **(Figures 3.45, 3.46)**.

Follow Through

Once the ball is released towards the target, the outfielder should finish his or her throwing mechanics by allowing their arm to decelerate naturally and come to rest just outside the stride-foot knee. The back foot will release off the ground, heel to the sky, and eventually

FIGURE 3.47

Outfielders should follow through, allowing the throwing arm to finish beside the front knee while maintaining momentum to the target.

finish forward in front of the stride foot. This process allows the outfielder's hips to finish rotating; momentum continues forward towards the target even though the ball is gone **(Figure 3.47)**.

Work through the following drills and practice ideas to reinforce good outfield mechanics.

Specific Outfield Drills

 Refer to Player-Pitch (Ages 9–10) "Outfield Drills" on the DVD for the following drills:

A. Tree—Improves an outfielder's drop step, approach angle, route to the ball, and ability to work through fly balls and ground balls.
B. Tennis racket—Improves an outfielder's ability to adjust to a ball in flight.
C. Fly ball patterns—Improves outfielders' abilities to run down a fly ball, run softly on their feet, adjust their positioning to a ball in flight, and set their feet once the ball is caught.

Additional Outfield Practice

A. Teach outfielders to practice crow hops by placing a ball in their glove and getting into a fly ball receiving position with their throwing-side foot behind them. Tell outfielders to place their caps on the ground just in front of their front (or glove-side) foot. On the coach's command, they should execute a crow hop by driving the back foot up and over the cap while transitioning the ball from the glove to the throwing hand. The body should finish in a power position.
B. When implementing drills or any practice ideas, players should take turns being the cut-off person in order for outfielders to practice throwing to an infielder (who will catch and relay the ball to the target in an actual game).
C. Ask players to work on their drop step and crossover step by following the command of an adult. Instruct the outfielder to creep into a ready position. If you want him or her to execute a drop step, point to the area where the ball would be hit. The outfielder should open his or her body quickly and accelerate in that general direction while keeping their eyes on you. If you want them to work on a crossover step, point directly to your side or towards the infield. In either case, the outfielder would take a crossover step and accelerate in that general direction.

PITCHING MECHANICS

This is usually the age group when players begin to pitch in actual games instead of batting off of a coach or a machine. This new element of the game provides a significant challenge to coaches who need to instruct players on basic pitching mechanics in order to help them throw consistent strikes. It takes more than a good arm to become a competent pitcher, although a strong arm helps. The key is to find those who can consistently repeat the basic phases of the delivery. Throwing a baseball overhand is an unnatural process for the human arm. Therefore, you must take precautions not to put a player at risk by allowing them to pitch too often. Coaches can get caught up in the trap of wins and losses, and the emotional rush of competing can result in a loss of perspective to the detriment of the pitcher.

Pitchers' arms and bodies need adequate time to recover between outings. It is a delicate balance between rest and throwing that actually builds up arm strength to adequately handle the demands of pitching. To keep pitching mechanics as simple as possible, players can be taught to implement "stretch mechanics," which are typically used at older ages to prevent base runners from easily stealing a base. Simplified mechanics reduce a pitcher's margin of error—fewer body movements are needed to create good balance and good lateral movement. Both elements are necessary to execute a consistent delivery to the plate.

 Refer to Player-Pitch (Ages 9–10) "Pitching Mechanics" on the DVD for detailed interactive instruction.

The following is the minimum skill progression needed for nine- and ten-year-olds to pitch using stretch mechanics.

Pitching from the Stretch: Engage the Rubber and Sign

The pitcher creates a good athletic position by placing the back foot parallel and centered against the pitcher's rubber. The front foot should be farther than shoulder-width from the back foot and aimed directly to the point of home plate. The player's hands can be relaxed at his or her side, with the ball in the throwing hand, or the player can lean slightly forward, resting the glove against the front thigh. The player should glance at the catcher's hand to receive the sign so he or she knows what type of pitch to throw, for instance, fastball or changeup **(Figure 3.48)**.

FIGURE 3.48

The pitcher should set up against the rubber before looking for the sign from the catcher.

FIGURE 3.49

The pitcher should create a good set position, with the throwing hand and the glove pausing somewhere between the chin and waist.

Set Position

To create a proper set position, the pitcher should move his or her front foot closer to the back foot to narrow their center of gravity while bringing both hands together to meet in the center of their body. Hands should intersect somewhere between the pitcher's chin and their waist. The player should pause in this position for a split second to get balanced and controlled. Eyes should be focused on the catcher's mitt **(Figure 3.49)**.

Balance Point

To create a balance point, the pitcher should raise his or her front knee to a comfortable position somewhere around waist-high; the knee should be turned in slightly towards the center of the body. This action closes and loads the hips, providing additional power. To sync tempo between the lower body and upper body, the pitcher's hands should mirror the action of the front knee during the knee lift and/or the descent. For example, if the pitcher's hands start low in their set position, they should come up as the knee rises, and go down when the knee descends. Conversely, if the pitcher prefers his or her hands high in their set position, he or she should keep them still on the knee lift and then drop them when the knee falls.

During the lift and descent of the front knee, that ankle should remain relaxed and close to the back knee. The pitcher's head should be aligned with the navel, and the player is now in a loaded position, balanced over his or her back leg. **(Figure 3.50)**.

Create Direction into the Power Position

As a pitcher's hands follow the front knee down, they should eventually separate near the navel. This initiates an equal and opposite movement of the arms. As the thumb of the gloved hand works down, forward, and up, finishing where the glove-arm elbow is pointed at the catcher, the thumb of the throwing hand works down, back, and up, finishing with the back elbow shoulder-high, with the ball pointed away from the target. In the power position, the pitcher's throwing elbow creates a backwards "L". Simultaneously, the lower body creates direction by striding directly to the plate, leading with the outside of the heel in order to keep the hips closed and loaded as long as possible. The stride foot will eventually rotate so the toes are pointed at the plate just before the foot lands on the clay. The player's eyes should be focused on the catcher's mitt. The pitcher is now in the power position **(Figure 3.51)**.

FIGURE 3.50

Pitchers should raise their front knee while loading the pelvis to create good balance during delivery.

FIGURE 3.51

The pitcher should create good direction to the plate while putting the upper body in a power position.

FIGURE 3.52

The pitcher begins the throw by keeping the throwing elbow shoulder-high.

FIGURE 3.53

This pitcher achieves extension while maintaining good posture with the glove side.

Throw and Extension

These two phases of the pitch happen very quickly. The pitcher should accelerate the baseball from behind his or her body to the release point out in front of the body while simultaneously moving his or her head towards the target. During the throw, the player's glove-arm elbow should transition from pointing at the target to a position beside the hip. The pitcher's lower body puts energy into the pitch by pushing off the rubber with the back leg, which creates momentum and accelerates the hips into rotation. The pitcher should extend the throwing hand completely towards the catcher's mitt to release the ball, snapping his or her wrist hard to create backwards, or twelve-o'clock to six-o'clock, rotation. Teach pitchers to visualize that they are throwing through a narrow hallway to the point of the plate: neither their body parts nor the ball should hit the imaginary walls **(Figures 3.52, 3.53)**.

Follow Through

Once the pitcher releases the ball to the catcher's mitt, he or she should finish the mechanics by allowing the throwing arm to decelerate naturally and come to rest just outside their stride-foot knee. Simultaneously, the glove-arm elbow continues to move from beside the hip to behind the hip so the throwing shoulder can end up pointed at the target. The back foot will release off the ground, heel to the sky, and eventually finish forward beside or past the stride foot. This process allows the hips to finish rotating and return to a position to field the ball, if it's hit back to the pitcher **(Figure 3.54)**.

Work through the following pitching drills and practice ideas to reinforce good delivery mechanics.

FIGURE **3.54**

To finish the delivery, the pitcher's throwing arm should naturally come to a stop just outside the stride-foot knee.

Specific Pitching Drills

 Refer to Player-Pitch (Ages 9–10) "Pitching Drills" on the DVD for the following drills:

A. Coach hand-off—Improves a pitcher's ability to create a good balance point and hold it before making the pitch.
B. Coach toss balance—Reinforces the pitcher's balance point before he or she commits to creating direction in the delivery.
C. Towel—Emphasizes the extension element of the pitch.
D. Bucket—Improves knee lift, balance, and hip loading.
E. Pitchers T—Improves direction of the stride foot to the plate. (Do not confuse this with the Hitter's Tee drill.)

Additional Pitching Practice

A. Dry mechanics—Adults should take extra time to lead pitchers through the phases of the stretch delivery step-by-step without a baseball. The focus should be on completing each segment correctly. The steps include setup, set position, balance point, power position, extension, and finish.
B. Pitchers should be given side work or a bullpen during practice or at home to provide needed repetitions to improve muscle memory

in their delivery mechanics. If there is an extra person available, make him or her wear a batter's helmet and stand in the right-handed and left-handed batter's box with a bat. This helps pitchers mentally prepare for a time when a hitter will be standing in the box during a game.

C. During practice, pitchers should take part in simulated games or modified scrimmages to mentally prepare to throw against hitters in a real game. This helps pitchers learn that once they throw the ball to the plate, there are other responsibilities such as fielding their position and backing up bases in the event of errant throws.

TYPES OF PITCHES

It is tough to win games at any level if pitchers struggle with their fastball. The fastball is the most elementary pitch in baseball. Pitchers of any age should first develop their ability to consistently throw this pitch for a strike. They should then learn the keys to effectively throwing a changeup. This combination of a faster pitch and a slower pitch should be enough to keep hitters off balance. If you find a pitching prospect at the age of nine and ten who can consistently throw a fastball and changeup for a strike, you have a very special player! Under no circumstances should players this age be taught or be allowed to throw a curveball because they can sustain serious elbow or shoulder injuries as a result. Position players who also pitch should alternate their grips when they are performing throwing drills, playing catch, or throwing long. They must get comfortable with the feel of each grip and how it affects the ball when they release it. There is more than one way to grip a baseball to throw certain pitches. Therefore, players should tweak their grips to determine which works best for them. Coaches should also begin to educate their players on the mental side of pitching. It is a skill in itself for young players to appropriately handle their negative emotions, which can surface from struggling to learn how to throw a certain pitch or from disappointing performances in a game. The pitcher is the only player on defense who gets to hold the ball on every play. Pitchers are a major factor in a game and the center of attention for other players, as well as for the fans. This can put a lot of pressure on a little person who is trying his or her best but having a bad day on the diamond.

 Refer to Player-pitch (Ages 9–10) "Pitching Grips" on the DVD for detailed interactive instruction.

The following are the grips needed for nine- and ten year-old players to pitch a baseball.

Four-Seam Fastball

The first grip that coaches should teach a pitcher is the four-seam fastball. This is the easiest pitch to throw for a strike. If released properly, four laces of the ball rotate through the air, helping to keep the throw in line with the target. To properly execute a four-seam grip, pitchers should hold the baseball with their pointer and middle finger on the top laces or seams of the baseball. The pads of these two fingers rest across the seams. The thumb should be underneath the ball and approximately midway between the distance of the top two fingers. The ring finger and pinkie finger rest on the side of the ball to give it balance **(Figures 3.55, 3.56)**.

Two-Seam Fastball

Once a pitcher can command the four-seam fastball for a strike, it is time to introduce the player to a two-seam fastball. This will create some movement and deception to fool the hitter. The main variation from the four-seam fastball is how the laces or seams of the ball are positioned in the fingers. When a two-seam fastball is properly released, the ball cuts through the air, moving naturally from right to left or left to right. Some pitchers have trouble controlling this for a strike because the ball can

FIGURE **3.55**

Front view of a four-seam grip of a fastball.

FIGURE **3.56**

Side view of a four-seam grip of a fastball.

FIGURE 3.57

Front view of a two-seam fastball.

FIGURE 3.58

Side view of a two-seam fastball.

start off in the strike zone and drift out by the time it reaches the plate. Additional movement can be created with a two-seam fastball by holding the ball slightly off center, adjusting thumb placement, or holding the ball next to the seams instead of placing the pads of the fingers directly on the seams (**Figures 3.57, 3.58**).

Changeup

The final pitch that should be introduced to this age group is a changeup. This pitch is meant to deceive the hitter by looking like a fastball on release but, in actuality, it is 10 to 15 miles per hour slower. The arm speed and action of the pitcher will convince the hitter he or she is seeing a fastball, however, by the time they realize it is a changeup, it will be too late. The batter will either swing early and miss or hit the ball softly to the defense. For a changeup grip, the ball is held deeper in the hand or the palm than a fastball. The index finger slides off to the thumb side of the ball and the pinkie raises up on the opposite side of the ball. This grip is referred to as a "circle change" or "O.K. change" because of the position of the hand. The changeup is a feel (touch) pitch, and it can be difficult for some players to throw a consistent strike using this grip (**Figures 3.59, 3.60**).

Implement the following to reinforce proper pitching grips.

Specific Ideas to Reinforce Pitching Grips

A. Encourage pitchers to alternate a four-seam grip, two-seam grip, and changeup grip when executing throwing drills or playing catch.

FIGURE 3.59

Front view of a "circle" or "O.K." changeup grip.

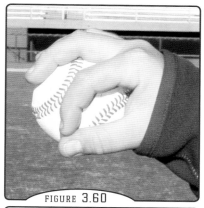

FIGURE 3.60

Side view of a "circle" or "O.K." changeup grip.

B. Suggest that pitchers implement a four-seam grip, two-seam grip, and changeup grip when executing specific pitching drills.

C. Encourage pitchers to alternate using a changeup grip with fastball grips when throwing long. This helps players maintain good arm speed with the grip, which is essential to throwing a good changeup.

D. Guessing game—Pitchers should vary their grips when throwing with an adult. The adult should try to correctly identify the grip used for every throw. The goal of the pitcher is to make it difficult for the adult to identify the grip based on the release of the ball. Difference in ball speed and/or movement should be how the adult can determine the grip or type of pitch.

CATCHER MECHANICS

Catchers are considered to be the anchor of a team's defense. They embody team leadership, contribute to the pace of the game, and provide confidence to their pitcher. A skilled catcher keeps the game moving at a good pace, which helps the defense stay focused on making plays. A good catcher can effectively block pitches thrown in the dirt, which gives the pitcher added confidence to throw a changeup with a runner on third base. If your league permits stealing bases, a good catcher can prevent base runners from freely taking the next base, which can deflate the momentum of the opponents. Coaches should provide adequate practice time to work with their catchers on the skills of receiving, blocking, throwing to bases, and retrieving wild pitches.

Refer to Player-Pitch (Ages 9–10) "Catcher Mechanics" on the DVD for detailed interactive instruction.

The following is the minimum skill progression needed for nine- and ten-year-olds to play the position of catcher.

Position to the Hitter

Teach the catcher how to create the proper distance from the hitter to avoid being hit with a bat on the swing. The catcher should be far enough to be just out of reach of the batter's back leg **(Figure 3.61)**.

Giving Signs Stance

Teach catchers the correct stance for giving the pitcher their signals. Signals tell the pitcher what kind of pitch the catcher wants him or her to throw. The keys to this stance include narrowing the distance between the catcher's knees so only the pitcher and middle infielders can see the signals. The catcher's hand should be against the middle seam of his or her pants, deep in the crotch. The catcher's fingers should not extend below the crotch, where they could be seen from behind. The mitt should be open and resting next to the left shin to prevent the third base coach from stealing the pitch signs by looking in from the side **(Figure 3.62)**.

FIGURE 3.61

The catcher must be positioned far enough behind a batter to avoid being hit by a poor swing, yet close enough to effectively catch strikes.

FIGURE 3.62

The catcher's hand signal should be given deep between the legs to prevent it from being seen by the offensive team.

FIGURE 3.63

This catcher has assumed a primary receiving stance.

FIGURE 3.64

Catchers should protect their throwing hand by hiding it behind their ankle.

Primary Receiving Stance

Teach catchers to create a basic receiving stance with knees bent, feet outside the knees, toes pointed slightly out, and weight on the inside of the feet. Catchers should extend their glove-side elbow beyond their knees to give the pitcher a good target. This also allows the catcher to receive the ball in front of the body with a relaxed arm and wrist. The player should catch the pitch by controlling the baseball; the ball should not move the glove backwards. This gives the umpire a better look at the pitch. It is critical that catchers learn to protect their throwing hand from being hit by a stray baseball. Teach them to hide their throwing hand behind their ankle **(Figures 3.63, 3.64)**.

Secondary Receiving Stance

If stealing bases is allowed and runners occupy first and/or second base, teach catchers how to adjust their positioning into a secondary stance. There are few simple variations of the primary catching stance that reduce the time it takes to throw the baseball to second or third base, giving the catcher an advantage. Catchers should slightly stagger their feet so the throwing foot is slightly behind the glove-side foot. They should slightly raise their buttocks to be in a better position to quickly accelerate into a power position to make a throw. To make a quick transition, their throwing hand should come from behind the ankle but be kept at a safe distance directly behind the mitt to protect it from a foul tip. Once the pitch is received, the catcher must quickly use basic throwing mechanics to transition into a power position and rapidly release the ball to the target base **(Figures 3.65, 3.66, 3.67)**.

FIGURE 3.65

Catchers should use their secondary receiving stance if base runners are allowed to steal bases and there are runners on first and/or second base.

FIGURE 3.66

In a secondary stance, catchers should stagger their feet, raise their buttocks, and protect their throwing hand by placing it behind their mitt.

FIGURE 3.67

Catchers should stay low as they achieve a good power position to throw.

Blocking a Pitch on Center

Part of a catcher's responsibility is learning how to effectively handle pitches that bounce. Catchers should be taught, through repetitive drills, how to react correctly to a baseball pitched in the dirt directly in front of them. They should instinctively fall forward to their knees and tuck their chin into their chest protector. This decreases the relative angle of the ball they are trying to stop with their body, and prevents the ball from getting by them as a passed ball or wild pitch. Catchers should quickly fill the 5-hole (the empty space created between the legs when catchers falls to their knees) with an open glove while protecting the bare hand from being hit by the baseball by placing it behind the glove. The goal is to let the chest protector cushion the impact of the ball so it falls in front of the catcher. Once the baseball is blocked, the catcher should quickly get to his or her feet and retrieve the ball with the throwing hand (Figure 3.68).

FIGURE 3.68

Catchers should create an effective blocking position to handle a pitch thrown in the dirt directly in front of them.

FIGURE 3.69

The catcher should create an effective blocking position to handle a pitch thrown in the dirt off to the side.

Blocking an Off-Center Pitch

Coaches should use drills to introduce the skill of blocking balls in the dirt to either side of the catcher. This requires more coordination, confidence, and body control. As soon as the catcher determines that the ball will bounce in the dirt to his or her side, he or she must drive the knee closest to the ball down at an angle, while simultaneously pushing with the opposite foot. This action swings the catcher's body around the ball while reducing the angle of the block. The catcher should lean forward, tuck the chin into his or her chest protector, and curl the shoulders in to form a soft pillow to absorb the impact of the ball and keep it in front of him or her **(Figure 3.69)**.

Passed Balls or Wild Pitch Retrieval

If base runners are allowed to advance on passed balls and wild pitches, coaches should teach their catchers how to efficiently retrieve a ball that gets by them, especially if there is a base runner at third base who may attempt to score. Once catchers recognize that the ball has gotten by them, they should quickly spring to their feet and run full speed after it. The pitcher should point in the direction of the ball, just in case the catcher did not see where it rebounded from the attempted block. The catcher should slide feet-first to the side of the ball, field the ball, and while rising on his or her knees, throw it to the pitcher, who will be covering the plate for the tag **(Figures 3.70, 3.71)**.

FIGURE 3.70

On a passed ball or wild pitch with base runners at third, the catcher must learn to slide and retrieve the ball in one motion.

FIGURE 3.71

Once the ball is retrieved, the catcher must learn to transition to his or her knees and throw the ball in one motion.

Work through the following drills and practice ideas to reinforce good catcher mechanics.

Specific Catcher Drills

 Refer to Player-Pitch (Ages 9–10) "Catcher Drills" on the DVD for the following drills:

A. Receiving tennis balls—Improves the mechanics and confidence of catching a pitch with control behind the plate.
B. Block and recover—Improves the mechanics and confidence of blocking a baseball pitched in the dirt.
C. Blocking variety—Improves the mechanics of blocking baseballs that are off to the catcher's side.
D. Passed ball—Improves the mechanics of retrieving passed balls or wild pitches and then throwing the ball to the pitcher covering the plate.

Additional Catcher Practice

A. Adults can throw baseballs to the catcher, who receives the simulated pitch with his or her mitt, squeezing it to maintain control.
B. Adults can use a pitching machine (if one is available) to give catchers many repetitions to work on both a primary receiving

stance and a secondary receiving stance in which they must catch the ball and throw to second or third base.

C. Ask catchers to put on full gear and get behind the plate during batting practice to become accustomed to catching and blocking the ball when a batter swings and misses, does not swing at a pitch, or the ball is thrown in the dirt. This will also give catchers experience throwing the ball back to the mound.

D. Adults should encourage catchers to practice their receiving skills by controlling the baseball when they are performing their throwing drills or playing catch.

E. Coaches should make sure catchers work with pitchers in the bullpens or when they get their side work. Do not let catchers get lazy with their receiving and blocking skills during this time.

F. Catchers should participate in practice games or modified scrimmages to learn how to receive the baseball and block the baseball with actual hitters in the batter's box.

FUNDAMENTAL OFFENSE SKILLS FOR PLAYER-PITCH BASEBALL: HITTING

Offensive skills at this level of baseball include hitting and baserunning. However, the primary focus of this section will be to address hitting mechanics. It is very important that players learn to consistently execute the whole-body movement patterns needed to correctly swing a bat. If coaches or parents fail to address swing flaws, they are allowing the brain and nervous system of young players to be falsely programmed.

The player-pitch level of baseball is the first time most hitters will officially bat off a pitcher their own age. Some players may be afraid of being hit with the pitch— they must overcome this fear. Coaches should continue to build on the fundamental hitting skills that were introduced at the coach- or machine-pitch level. Players are now physically stronger, have more experience, and are able to refine hitting drills they learned when they were seven and eight. Therefore, coaches should begin to focus on improving smaller elements of the swing within the general phases of stance, load and stride, power position, contact, extension, and finish.

To be a complete hitter, a player must eventually conquer the three aspects of hitting. The first element is swing mechanics, which is the physical process of swinging the bat at the ball. The second element is pitch recognition—the ability to recognize correct spin, speed, and location of a pitch. The last element includes the ability to develop a plan of attack and then to make necessary adjustments from pitch to pitch, at-bat to at-bat, and from game to game.

Some coaches and parents think hitting is just swinging a bat at the ball. When they learn the intricacies within the phases, they may try to impart too much information at one time to their hitters. Avoid overwhelming a hitter with too many adjustments at once—this can paralyze learning and significantly slow progress. Focus on large swing flaws first, using drills to reinforce proper muscle memory. Once a problem has been successfully addressed, move on to other concerns. Your hitters should focus on being ready to hit strikes and swinging at good pitches. Also, they should be taught how to make a discernable two-strike adjustment by widening their stance, shortening up on the bat, and cutting down their swing to get the baseball in play instead of taking a big swing and striking out.

 Refer to Player-Pitch (Ages 9–10) "Hitting Mechanics" on the DVD for detailed interactive instruction.

The following is the minimum skill expectation for nine- and ten-year-old players to swing a bat correctly.

Proper Grip for Hitting
Teach your players how to grip the bat by lining up the door-knocking knuckles of the four fingers of each hand (minus the thumbs). It is very important for hitters to hold the bat in their hands where the fingers meet the palms. This is where they are strongest and will generate the most quickness, power, and control of the bat when they swing **(Figure 3.72)**.

Stance
Teach your players how to achieve an athletic stance with feet slightly wider apart than shoulder-width, knees and hips slightly flexed, weight slightly forward, with the head just over the toes. The player's head should be straight up and down, with both eyes focused on the pitcher. The batter should raise his or her hands into a position approximately six inches off their back shoulder. Both elbows should be relaxed and pointing down. The angle of the bat should not be extreme, for instance, not pointed straight up, parallel to the ground, or wrapped behind the hitter's head. The goal is to take a short, compact swing to the ball, and extreme bat angles can make a swing long and decrease consistent contact with the ball. Teach

FIGURE 3.72

Teach players how to check their grip of the bat so they can increase their chance of executing a quick swing.

FIGURE 3.73

The hitter should prepare by getting into an athletic batting stance that avoids extreme angles and movements.

players to add some rhythm or slight movement into their stance. It is easier to start a swing if the body is already in motion, instead of static; slight motion helps to relax muscles, and relaxed muscles are fast muscles (**Figure 3.73**).

Load and Stride

Teach your players how to progress from their stance to a loaded position in which they are in the best posture to attack the ball. When the ball is about to be released to the plate by the pitcher, the hitter should lift his or her front foot and take a stride of a few inches forward towards the pitcher. He or she should land on the big toe and the ball of the stride foot to keep weight from transferring forward. The heel of the stride foot should be an inch or two off the clay. Simultaneously, or just before the stride, the hitter should load the upper body by slightly moving both hands away from the pitcher to a position behind the back shoulder and directly over the back foot. This position is often referred to as the "knockout slot" and puts the body in a strong position to swing the bat. Once the stride foot lands, the hitter's head should stay relatively still through the swing to provide the best chance of seeing the pitch. Coaches must teach hitters this concept of "load and stride" to create a good posture position to prepare to hit the ball (**Figure 3.74**).

FIGURE 3.74

Players should be taught how to load and stride to be in a stronger position to attack the pitch.

FIGURE 3.75

The hitter begins his swing by initiating a short "power" move-ment with the knob of the bat while moving the back knee a few inches towards the pitched baseball.

Power

Teach your hitters to let the ball travel from the pitcher's hand through space to the plate before they swing the bat. When the hitter decides to attack a pitch, the heel of his or her front foot should drop to the clay. This engages the batter's upper and lower body into the swing process. The knob on the small end of the bat controls the barrel of the bat. This means the barrel follows where the knob goes in the swing. Thus, in order for the barrel to take a short path to connect with the ball, the batter must initiate the swing by driving the knob down directly at the inside part of the baseball. Attempting to hit the inside of the ball (instead of the back center of the ball) indirectly helps the hitter generate more bat head speed. Simultaneously, the batter should engage the lower half of the body into the swing by moving the back kneecap a few inches towards the baseball **(Figure 3.75)**. It's as if the hands on the bat and the back kneecap are tied together for the first several inches of the swing. As the back knee starts toward the ball, the back heel will begin to rotate off the ground distributing the portion of the hitter's weight to the back leg, resting on the edge of the big toe (the inside of the foot) .

Contact

Although it is very hard to see with the naked eye, on contact with the baseball, the hand at the knob of the bat should be in a palm-down

FIGURE 3.76

As this hitter makes contact with the baseball, he or she is in a strong posture position with hands palm up and palm down.

FIGURE 3.77

For the greatest chance of hitting the ball hard, hitters should achieve full extension through the hitting zone with the barrel of the bat.

(towards the ground) position and the hand higher up on the bat should be palm up (towards the sky). The hitter's back elbow should be near the side of his or her hip, and the back arm should be bent in an "L" position. The front arm should be slightly bent but firm. The batter's front knee should also be slightly bent but can be straight. The stride foot should be turned in and the hitter should be balanced. The back heel should be pointed up to release the hips into full rotation **(Figure 3.76)**.

Extension Phase

Teach your hitters to "get extension of the barrel through the ball." This keeps the barrel of the bat in the hitting zone longer, and gives the hitter more room for error. For example, a batter should visualize hitting seven baseballs in a line back to back. The goal of the hitter's swing is to be "short and quick to the inside of the ball" and then to "get extension in order to stay through the ball." This is referred to as "short to and long through." A hitter who initiates the swing correctly but prematurely moves the bat head out of the hitting area before achieving full extension of the barrel is dramatically decreasing the chances of consistently hitting the ball hard **(Figure 3.77)**.

Finish

Teach your hitter how to finish the swing in a balanced way. The hitter's head should be aligned between the middle of the feet, and eyes should be horizontal, focused on where contact was made with the ball. The hands should finish the swing near the height of the front shoulder with the bat behind the hitter. It is best to keep both hands on the bat (instead of removing the top hand from the bat). If contact is made with the ball, the hitter should run hard to first base. The player's weight is supported equally by the stride foot and on the inside big toe of the back foot **(Figure 3.78)**.

FIGURE 3.78

The hitter should finish the swing balanced, with the head and eyes still focused on where contact was made with the ball.

Work through the following drills and practice ideas to reinforce good swing mechanics.

Specific Hitting Drills

 Refer to Player-Pitch (Ages 9–10) "Hitting Drills" on the DVD for the following drills:

A. Basic tee—Improves the fundamental swing mechanics of a hitter.
B. Double tee—Creates a good swing plane or bat path to the baseball with an emphasis on extension.
C. High tee— Helps hitters to create a correct swing path to the baseball.
D. Basketball tee—Helps hitters to create good extension through the ball.
E. Noodle tee—Helps hitters to create a short swing path to the ball.
F. Front foot platform—Prevents hitters from lunging or jumping at the ball.

Additional Hitting Practice

A. Side toss—Adults can set up a station where they kneel off to the side of a hitter at a 45-degree angle. They can toss the ball underhand to the player, who hits the ball into a net. If it is a bad feed, the hitter should watch the simulated pitch go by. It is critical that adults make good feeds so they are not creating flaws when the child is trying to hit the ball. The goal is to enforce proper swing mechanics; therefore, the feeder must not be in a hurry and rapid-fire one feed right after the next. If it is a bad feed, the hitter should take the pitch; this means not to swing but to wait for a good feed.

B. Front toss—Adults can set up a protective screen, such as an L-screen, directly in front of and a short distance away from the hitter to ensure accuracy. Feed a firm underhand toss to the hitter from the side of the screen (making sure to keep your hand and body behind the screen to avoid being hit with a batted ball). This allows the batter to swing at strikes from a similar angle as he or she would see in the game. It is a great way to elicit many swings in a short time and to build confidence.

C. Batting practice from the coach and/or a batting machine—Simply throw batting practice or use a pitching machine to provide extra opportunities for players to hit the ball.

D. Film hitters—Adults can set up a video camera to tape each player taking three to five swings. Play back the video frame by frame to help expose flaws that cannot be discerned with the naked eye.

PLAYER-PITCH 101: TEACHING GAME SKILLS

Game play at the player-pitch level is more competitive than at younger levels, and coaches and players alike are looking to gain an advantage to score runs and win games. In order for a team to compete successfully, coaches must prepare their players for basic situations that can arise when playing an opponent. Below is a simple list of offensive and defensive skills and situations that should be mastered by the team before they graduate from the player-pitch level. Use practice time and games to reinforce these essential skills.

Team Offense—The Basics

Teach your players the following:

1. How to decode or "read" the signs typically given from the third base coach to the hitter before every pitch.

2. How to run the bases aggressively to force the defense to throw and catch under pressure.

3. When batting, how to correctly make a two-strike adjustment in order to put the baseball in play instead of swinging freely, which

often results in a strike out. Putting the ball in play forces the defense to execute a catch and/or throw, and many times the batter will reach base due to an error, or a base runner can advance, which can help their team score runs and win games.

4. How to take a lead from first or second base and read pitchers' fundamental basic pick-off attempts (if the league allows leads, base stealing, and pick-off attempts).

5. How to round first base and take an aggressive turn on a base hit through the infield to the outfield.

6. How to understand the difference between a force and non-force situation when advancing to the next base.

7. When and how base runners tag up at third base on a fly ball to the outfield.

8. How to execute a feet-first slide.

9. When players must return to their original base on fly balls caught in the air with less than two outs.

10. How to correctly look at or listen to first and third base coaches about when to stop at the current base or continue on to the next base.

11. How to avoid being tagged in a rundown by the defense.

Note that coaches must keep order, organization, and safety in the dugout. The discipline and routines that are needed to control your team are established at practice.

Team Defense—The Basics

Teach your players:

1. To know, between pitches, how many outs there are and where they will throw the ball if it is hit to them in the air or on the ground.

2. What constitutes a force out and how to execute a force out at all bases.

3. When it is necessary to tag out a base runner instead of throwing to a base to execute a force play.

4. How to properly tag base runners when they are sliding into a base.

5. Simple cut-off and relay scenarios when making plays in the outfield and throwing the ball back into the infield to prevent runners from advancing to extra bases.

6. How the first baseman should hold base runners at first base (if leads and/or stealing are allowed in your league).

7. How pitchers execute basic pick-off moves to first and second bases to hold base runners close and make it more difficult for them to steal bases.

8. How middle infielders can hold base runners close to second base and how to execute basic pick-off attempts.

9. How middle infielders and third basemen can move from their position to cover the base when runners are trying to steal a base (if stealing bases is allowed in your league).

10. How to properly communicate on fly ball priority. This helps players aggressively track down fly balls without being afraid to collide with a teammate.

11. How to execute basic rundown scenarios between all bases.

12. How to execute basic cut-offs and relays between the infield and outfield.

13. How to defend against "first and third" situations implemented by the offense. These situations will be used by many teams to score runs and cause havoc for the defense.

14. How to execute a basic rundown in which an offensive player is caught by the defense between two bases.

15. How, when, and where the pitcher should back up bases when balls are hit to the outfield.

16. How the pitcher should cover first base when a ground ball is hit to the first baseman so he or she can flip the ball to the pitcher for the force out.

17. How the pitcher should cover home on a passed ball or wild pitch that gets by the catcher.

18. How and where all outfielders need to be in order to back up throws to bases. There is a place for every player on every single play.

POST-GAME TALK

At the conclusion of each game, the head coach should bring the team together into a group in the outfield or just outside the field of play. This should be done without the parents of the players, who can distract the children. The coach should review some of the simple things that were learned from that game.

- Ask players to take a knee (kneel) and face the coaches, giving the coaches their full attention.
- Each coach on staff should share one or two quick points about the game that can help the team improve or let the team know what it needs to focus on at the next practice.
- Coaches should focus on the positive aspects of the game.
- Never single out a player for his or her mistakes. However, it is okay to use players as positive examples. Find good things to say about all your players, primarily placing emphasis on a strong team concept.
- Never blame losses on the umpires or any other external factor such as the field playing conditions, weather, and so on.
- Remind players of the next practice or game, even though most players won't remember. This teaches responsibility, and players will need this skill as they grow older.
- Bring the team together for a simultaneous dismissal where all players put their hands together and shout "Team!"

Ask parents to alternate bringing a team snack and drink to provide after each post-game talk.

Refer to Chapter 8, "Coaching Youth Baseball," for more ideas on how to conduct a productive and enjoyable baseball practice.

PART TWO

Outside the Lines

Coaches and parents who love kids and like baseball will want to help them maximize their experience, reach their full potential, and ultimately achieve the success that will warrant moving up to higher levels of the game. Motivation to help players improve may include playing on a recreation or travel team, winning a starting position in the lineup, or clinching a spot on the all-star team, to name a few.

This section of the book will provide critical information to help coaches and parents tackle problems found in young baseball players. Chapter 4 will help you identify and eliminate common bad habits that can be developed in the initial years of participation in baseball. Chapters 5 and 6 will provide you with the means of recognizing and fixing the twelve most common hitting and pitching flaws that coaches and parents will encounter in players from T-ball to ten years old.

The final chapter of this section, Chapter 7, will address the role of parents in youth baseball. Many well-intentioned parents will find themselves engulfed in their child's baseball experience, and a percentage will eventually lose perspective as to why they signed up their child to play the game in the first place. Whether it is living through the child or just wanting the best for their kid, both perspectives can be dangerous if not kept in check on a regular basis. Thus, it is critical for the overall experience of their son or daughter that parents keep amateur baseball in perspective.

CHAPTER 4

SEVEN STEPS TO ELIMINATE BAD HABITS

Myth #1: IF A PLAYER TAKES ONE LESSON A WEEK AT A BASEBALL ACADEMY, HE OR SHE WILL SUCCESSFULLY ELIMINATE MOST BAD HABITS OVER TIME.

Secret: *Taking baseball lessons is a positive step towards improvement. However, it takes more than one hitting, pitching, or fielding lesson a week to eliminate most bad habits. Players must spend a minimum of three days a week if they want to create the correct muscle memory to successfully perform a new skill. This can be accomplished at an academy, team practice, with a parent, or practicing on their own.*

Myth #2: IF A PLAYER PERFORMS A VARIETY OF HITTING DRILLS, HE OR SHE CAN ELIMINATE MOST WEAKNESSES AS A HITTER.

Secret: *If used for a specific purpose, hitting drills can significantly benefit a player. However, performing random hitting drills incorrectly can create more hitting problems than they fix. For a drill to be effective, the player must know how to perform it correctly and have a specific purpose in mind when choosing and using that drill.*

Myth #3: IMPROVING A PLAYER'S MECHANICAL FLAWS (BAD HABITS) WHEN HITTING OFF A BATTER'S TEE WILL SUCCESSFULLY ELIMINATE THAT SAME PROBLEM IN THE PLAYER'S SWING IN THE GAME.

Secret: *Proper use of the batting tee is one of the first ways to address and attempt to correct flaws in a batter's swing. However, swinging correctly with a stationary baseball does not mean that the flaw will be fully eliminated when the player reacts to a live pitch.*

KEEPING IT FUN FOR THE KIDS

Baseball is a game. Games are supposed to be fun. Umpires start each game by using the phrase "Play Ball," with an emphasis on the word "Play." If pitching, hitting, fielding, and running the bases are not fun, why would anyone want to play the game? Fortunately, executing these skills is fun, and that is why children and adults alike play baseball every day all across the world.

Unfortunately, there are many coaches and parents who make learning the necessary baseball skills feel like a job. If players are going to learn the game correctly and eliminate bad habits, they must have a good time, or they will soon avoid anything to do with baseball and find something else to do with their time.

The challenge is to keep the element of fun in the teaching and learning process. We live in a world that thrives on instant gratification or reward. We want to see significant improvements right away. Our modern way of thinking is not conducive to learning or re-learning baseball skills in which it can take weeks, months, or years to eliminate an old habit. It is very rare for a person of any age to correctly learn a skill the first time they are taught it. Yet, many coaches and parents think their team or child will be the exception to that rule, and they end up frustrated with the slow, gradual progress.

Other coaches and parents take on the role of drill sergeant and treat their team, players, or children like they are in the military. They yell at their players, thinking it will make them try harder and learn faster. Wrong! Yelling only makes learning baseball feel like a job. Coaches and parents must have patience and provide encouragement. They must understand and be able to implement the skills necessary to eliminate a bad habit. The reward will be a smiling, more confident child who wants to play the game of baseball for years to come.

The Major Obstacle

Some players who possess bad habits can still achieve success in baseball, especially at the lower levels. It can be a major obstacle to convince a player, or his or her parents, to make skill changes when the player is currently experiencing success. To further complicate this challenge, players who attempt to make changes at a coach's or parent's request may, in the short-term, fail more often than they did when they were performing the skill incorrectly. This leads to frustration, and many players will abandon attempts at long-term positive changes for temporary success. Young participants play baseball at levels where the game is very slow, thus, players can get away with incorrect habits and still have temporary success.

Joe Sottolano, Head Baseball Coach at The United States Military Academy at West Point (Army), states, "I believe kids are born with a natural movement pattern and that pattern is either further developed or altered throughout their baseball experience. It is in the best interest of that athlete to work hard on basic fundamentals within their movement pattern as early and often as possible. This will enable them to develop positive habits that will decrease their learning curve and maximize their potential as they get older."

It becomes vital that anyone working with young baseball players truly understands where each player's skill level should be, based upon his or her age, before trying to teach a baseball skill. Many baseball skills, such as hitting, can consist of complex movements for young players, and there are only certain elements within the complete skill that must be mastered by specific ages (see Chapters 1 through 3 for minimum skill expectations by age group). This is a true building process, and the foundation must be correctly set if the house will stand, weather-tested, in the years to come.

The Confidence Factor

A player or his or her parents must have confidence in the instructor who requests skill changes. It must be evident that the instructor knows what he or she is talking about in order to successfully convince the player, who is currently doing well, that failure awaits in the future if he or she doesn't make a permanent change soon. Not only that, but the longer the player waits to make the change, the harder it will be to eliminate the bad habit.

THE SEVEN STEPS TO ELIMINATING BAD HABITS

Baseball is a physically and mentally challenging game that requires the mastery and use of a variety of offensive and defensive skills. Swinging a bat, throwing a ball, and fielding a baseball successfully require good hand-eye coordination, along with the ability to specifically order movements of different body parts by transferring energy throughout a pattern from start to finish. Simply put, it does not take much for something to go wrong and for failure to occur.

Humans are superior to any machine; however, we can use a computer as an example of the learning and skill programming process. When we learn a skill for the first time, we program our brain and nervous system, which tells the muscles to operate in a particular way in a certain situation. It is a form of software. We teach our brain "if this happens then you react this way." If we execute the function over and over, whether the right way or wrong way, it will eventually become reactionary or instinctive (without thought). We no longer have to tell the brain what to do; it knows. We have now created a habit.

The problem is that if we program our brain incorrectly, it becomes very difficult to deprogram it, "remove the software," or trash the process. Even if you know you must perform a skill differently to make a positive change, every time you make an unfocused effort, the mind and body performs the process the way you originally programmed it. The longer you perform the function incorrectly, the deeper the memory will be rooted in the computer's inner workings (muscle memory). This is what it is like to eliminate a bad habit in baseball. It takes a conscious, long-term effort of continuous re-teaching and thousands of correct repetitions of the skill to remove the old muscle memory and permanently "download" the new muscle memory.

It requires a committed coach or caring parent to seek the knowledge, share the information, and exhibit the patience to let the learning process occur in a child over time. Learning and changing baseball habits can be thought of as more of a marathon than a sprint. There are generally seven steps that should be followed if a player is going to successfully make a permanent change in his or her muscle memory to eliminate a bad habit. The steps are logical but probably won't be completed without a sincere desire to make a change. Good coaching, with correct advice and positive reinforcement, can also speed up the process. If the skill is not being performed correctly, coaches can suggest drills or give feedback to rectify it.

Step #1: Study the Skill Process

Players, coaches, or parents must know the hows and whys of a specific baseball skill in order to make a permanent improvement. Take the time to read the skill sequence of specific defensive and offensive skills in Chapters 1 through 3 based on the age of your player or child, and reference the photos to visualize the essential movement phases. Then view the corresponding skill instruction section on the enclosed DVD. Watch the skill performed over and over to become familiar with the sequence and relevant terminology. This seems like a very short step, however, it

Apply Skills to the Game

Drills are worthless if a hitter does not transfer the successful skill to the actual game. Most young hitters have the initial tendency to revert to their previous swing mechanics when they see a live-pitched baseball thrown on a game field. Young players treat a baseball field like many golfers do a driving range. They just want to see how far they can hit the ball and they abandon sound swing mechanics and purpose.

THE TWELVE COMMON HITTING FLAWS

The twelve flaws that follow are the most common problems found with young players. When players graduate from ten-year-old-level baseball, they should be free of these significant deficiencies. They will have a greater chance of continued success at the higher levels and their coach will not have to spend valuable time re-teaching the fundamental skills. Thus, if coaches or parents can successfully educate themselves about these particular flaws and their accompanying drills, they will be able to assist children in reaching their full potential. Many of these flaws are simple problems, such as gripping the bat incorrectly or rotating the back foot improperly during a swing.

Note: Because of the young ages of the hitters, many of the suggested drills are very simple corrective procedures and these will be explained in detail. However, if a drill can be viewed on the accompanying DVD, you will be directed to the location of that drill.

Flaw #1: Improper Grip on the Bat

Description: The hitter steps into the batter's box to hit with hands incorrectly holding the bat.

Problem: An improper grip on the bat is the most fundamental problem a hitter can have **(Figure 5.1)**. It will ultimately result in inconsistent contact with the baseball, a slower swing, and increased failure rates.

FIGURE 5.1

This hitter is not gripping the bat correctly; his hands are over-rotated and too tight.

FIGURE 5.2

This hitter is using a proper grip; the door-knocking knuckles are close to being lined up and the fingers are relaxed.

Goal: Teach your hitter to hold the bat with his or her hands where the fingers meet the palms **(Figure 5.2)**. This is where the hands are strongest and it provides the greatest control of the bat. A simple checkpoint is to make sure the door-knocking knuckles are lined up (or very close to being lined up). The fingers should also stay relaxed until the actual start of the swing because relaxed muscles are fast muscles and tight muscles are slow muscles.

Drills:

1. Let the hitter knock on a piece of wood to recognize the door-knocking knuckles. These include all four fingers of each hand (not the thumbs).

2. Demonstrate that there is strength in a proper grip. Ask your hitter to put his or her pointer finger deep in the palm of the opposite hand, squeeze the finger, and pull it out of the palm. Then ask the hitter to take the pointer finger and place it in their opposite hand where the fingers meet the palm, squeeze, and try to pull the pointer finger out. It will be apparent the hitter has a stronger grip where the fingers meet the palm. This correct grip position is created when the hitter lines up the door-knocking knuckles.

3. Demonstrate how relaxed muscles are fast muscles. Ask your hitter to bring his or her middle finger and thumb together so they touch lightly. While in this position, ask the hitter to snap his or her wrist from back to front. It should snap quickly if the fingers are relaxed. Then ask the hitter to take the same two fingers and squeeze them tightly together. This creates tight muscles in the wrist that react more slowly. Ask the player to snap his or her wrist from back to front. The wrist will move very slowly. This proves to the hitter that a relaxed grip on the bat will provide faster reflexes to hit the ball.

4. Teach your hitters to create a simple routine to check for grip when they step into the batter's box to hit. A helpful routine would be to

step into the batter's box with the back foot (the one closest to the catcher) first and then check their grip before bringing their front foot in to complete their stance. They should practice this routine over and over until they become comfortable with checking for a correct grip.

Flaw #2: Poor Plate Coverage

Description: The hitter steps into the batter's box and sets up in a poor stance in relation to the plate. This will prevent him or her from making consistent solid contact with a pitch that is thrown over the plate.

Problem: The hitter's initial setup may be too far away from or too close to the plate based upon the hitter's size and the size of the bat. Thus, when the bat is swung, the barrel or the "sweet spot" will not adequately cover the plate to hit a pitch thrown over the plate **(Figure 5.3)**.

Goal: When entering the batter's box, the hitter should establish a routine to get into a stance that is the proper distance from the plate. This will allow the barrel of the bat to adequately cover the plate with a fundamentally sound swing. It is the responsibility of the hitter to be able to hit a pitch thrown over the inside, middle, or outside part of the plate. If an umpire is consistently calling pitches off the plate a strike, the hitter may need to adjust his or her plate coverage to be able to handle that pitch as well **(Figure 5.4)**.

FIGURE **5.3**

This hitter is setting up in his stance too far from the plate to allow for consistent plate coverage with a correct swing.

FIGURE **5.4**

This hitter is setting up in a batting stance that will allow for good plate coverage with a correct swing.

Drills:

1. Ask your players to step into the batter's box and get into their batting stance. Direct them to start their swing in slow motion and to freeze on "contact" where the barrel would meet the ball on a swing. From this point, ask them to lower the bat straight to the ground. Leave the bat on the ground and ask them to come out in front of the plate (in pitcher's view) to see if the barrel of the bat is covering the majority of the plate.

2. Teach your hitters to establish a routine when they enter the batter's box to hit. Instruct them to reach across to the opposite corner of the plate with the end of the bat. This will ensure that they have good plate coverage for hitting a ball that is thrown across the inside and outside part of home plate.

Flaw #3: Not Loading to Hit (Ages 9 and Up)

Description: The hitter is not gathering the big muscles to deliver a blow to the baseball. This would be accomplished by slightly shifting his or her weight and hands back to get into the knockout slot. This process is not vital for players four through eight years old.

FIGURE 5.5

This hitter will execute a swing without creating a loaded position.

Problem: Neglecting to load the body by shifting the weight against the back leg and moving the bat to a position over the back foot will cause a hitter to lose power. The hitter will tend to have a slower, weaker swing **(Figure 5.5)**.

Goal: The hitter should gather or "recruit" the big muscles of the shoulders, midsection, and buttocks to deliver a stronger blow to the baseball. The load can be performed simultaneously with or before the stride. The action of drawing a bow and arrow is very similar to the load phase in hitting; the player should pretend to pull the string back with the back arm to shoot the arrow and then place both hands together as if holding a bat. Another example of a loading action is a punch. Punching a weight bag, for example, requires drawing the arm and weight back to use the big muscles to deliver a strong blow **(Figure 5.6)**.

Drills:

1. Instruct your players to practice dry loads, which means completing the action without a pitched baseball. Make sure hitters know that they can stride at the same time as loading the upper body, or they can load the upper body and then stride (whichever is more comfortable). If they don't have a preference, suggest they perform the load with the stride. When hitters have completed their load, tell them to freeze and let the bat slowly slip

FIGURE **5.6**

This hitter will get into a loaded position before executing a swing.

through their hands down to the ground. If their hands are in the correct loaded position, the bat should be close to touching the toes of their back foot. Another key is that their front arm will be bent close to or slightly past 90 degrees at the conclusion of the load. If they are in a good loaded position with the lower body, their weight should be distributed close to 60/40, with 60 percent of the body weight on the back foot and 40 percent on the front foot.

2. Ask players to stand next to a wall or fence with their back foot parallel to and touching the base of the wall. Each player creates a batting stance as if the pitcher were going to throw directly at the wall. When you give the command to "load," the player should move his or her hands back to where they gently touch the wall and are directly over their back foot, while striding with the front foot a maximum of six inches away from the wall. This action stretches the midsection of the body and prepares it to uncoil into the swing. Again, the player can stride and load together or load and then stride. Either way, he or she should finish with a 60/40 (back leg/ front leg) weight distribution. Tell players to freeze in this position to get a proper feel for good balance and body posture. Note that

you must check that players can still see the pitcher with both eyes once they are loaded. Stand directly in front of them and ask them to close the eye closest to you. They should still see you clearly with the furthest eye, which can sometimes be blocked by the bridge of the player's nose.

Flaw #4: Balance Problems (Overstriding and/or Lunging)

Description: The hitter takes a long stride and most of his or her weight shifts prematurely to the front leg (the front side of body) before the swing occurs. Alternately, the hitter jumps at the ball, moving towards the pitcher to hit the ball, rather than letting the ball travel to the hitting zone.

Problem: The hitter will create a lot of unnecessary problems with his or her swing just from overstriding or lunging **(Figure 5.7)**. These include, but are not limited to, losing balance, excessively moving the head (or eyes), the inability to consistently hit off-speed pitches, and significant loss of power.

Goal: The batter should maintain good hitting posture and balance through the swing—head centered between the zone created by the feet and navel. In order to accomplish this, the hitter should take a short (just a few inches), slow, soft, and straight stride with the front foot. This helps keep his or her head and eyes still.

The hitter's stride foot must hit the ground early so the body has adequate time to perform the swing correctly without being rushed by the pitch. A short stride will help accomplish this goal. The hitter then wants to let the baseball travel from the pitcher to the hitting zone, where the hitter makes ideal contact with the ball. This keeps him or her from lunging at the ball. Checkpoints at the conclusion of a good swing include the foot in front of the knee in the forward leg, good overall balance, good body posture (the head aligned over the navel and centered between the legs), the back knee pointed to the baseball, back heel to the sky, and a high swing finish with the hands **(Figure 5.8)**.

FIGURE 5.7

This hitter has taken both a long stride and lunged at the pitch, creating a weak posture or batting position.

FIGURE 5.8

This hitter has executed a short stride with a load; this helps to prevent lunging at the baseball.

Drills:

Refer to Player-Pitch (Ages 9–10) "Hitting Drills [F]" on the DVD for the first drill:

1. Front-foot platform drill—To execute the front-foot platform drill, hitters place their stride foot on an elevated platform approximately 6 inches off the ground. They then perform whatever specific drill you are working on in this position. For example, they could execute tee work from this position or front toss, etc. The platform helps to keep a player's weight back and prevent overstriding or a lunge.

2. Stride-foot device drill—To execute the stride-foot device drill, a coach or parent places a 2 × 4 on the ground in front of the stride foot. When hitters stride, they should not make contact with the wood. This keeps their stride short. You can also use a tire for this drill. Hitters start with only their stride foot in a tire. They must execute a stride without stepping on and falling all over the tire.

3. Decoy pitch or feed—The coach or parent randomly holds onto the ball, instead of letting it go, to prevent the delivery of a pitch or feed in any hitting drill. Players who are overstriding or lunging will find themselves in a poor posture position and you can bring it to their attention.

Flaw #5: Barring Out

Description: The hitter straightens out the front arm (the arm closest to the pitcher) when loading or starting the swing to hit the ball.

Problem: When the front arm "bars out," it effectively removes a link in the arm by straightening the elbow, and this forms one long "bar." This action will inhibit the hitter from a short, quick swing to the baseball. The hitter will now have to perform a long sweeping action of the bat to the ball, which results in a slow swing and inconsistent contact **(Figure 5.9)**.

A hitter who bars out will have trouble hitting the baseball to all parts of the field. Barring out can also contribute to posture problems because the locked or "barred" front arm causes the back elbow to move away from the back hip. This is a weak position for the back elbow when the hitter makes contact with the ball.

Goal: The hitter should keep flexion (relaxed bend) in the front elbow to initiate the swing by driving the knob of the bat directly to the baseball. This action is necessary to have a short swing **(Figure 5.10)**.

FIGURE **5.9**

This hitter is barring out on his load, which will inhibit a correct swing.

FIGURE **5.10**

This hitter has maintained flexion in his front elbow, which will allow the bat to take a correct path to the ball.

138

Drills:

Refer to Player-Pitch (Ages 9–10) "Hitting Drills [E]" on the DVD for the first drill:

1. The noodle tee drill.

2. Instruct your hitters to practice dry loads and strides. On the command of coach or parent, the players execute 25 to 30 proper loads, finishing each load and stride phase of the swing in the correct position with flexion in the front elbow.

3. Instruct your hitters to practice dry loads, strides, and stabs. Simply add to the last phase in the previous step. After the load and stride, the hitter should initiate the start of the swing by driving ("stabbing") the knob to the ball while simultaneously moving the back knee to the baseball. This is accomplished by starting to rotate the back foot heel to the sky, which releases the back knee. The back foot should not lift off the ground or drag forward. The back knee mirrors the direction of the hands to the ball.

Flaw #6: Casting

Description: Not to be confused with barring, casting is when the hitter pushes his or her hands and bat away from the body before starting the swing.

Problem: Like Flaw #5, casting will result in a long swing around the ball **(Figure 5.11)**. The hitter will have trouble with the inside fastball and difficulty consistently getting the barrel of the bat to the ball (making square contact). The "push away" action of the hands (toward the other batter's box) makes it difficult to take the knob of the bat to the baseball. As a result, the hitter will have difficulty generating bat speed and hitting balls hard to all parts of the field. This is a slow, weak posture position when trying to hit a baseball consistently hard. If you are looking at the hitter from the front, you

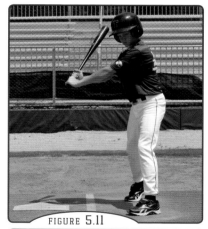

FIGURE 5.11

This hitter is casting the bat, which will result in a long, inefficient swing.

139

FIGURE 5.12

This hitter is taking the knob of the bat to the inside of the ball to create a short, efficient swing path.

will see a large space created between the chest and the hands with the bat as he or she "casts" the bat through the swing. Another indicator of a cast swing is that the hitter's back elbow will be away from the back hip on contact with the ball.

Goal: Every hitter should quickly get his or her body and hands into a strong position to make contact with the ball. If the hands are in the correct position, the bat is likely to be in the right position, too. A short, quick swing results when the knob of the bat can be driven to the pitched baseball and the hitter can maintain good posture, bringing the back elbow near the side of the hip at contact **(Figure 5.12)**.

Drills:

 Refer to Player-Pitch (Ages 9–10) "Hitting Drills [E]" on the DVD for the first drill:

1. The noodle tee drill.

2. Instruct your hitters to practice dry load, stride, and stabs, as described in Flaw 5, above.

3. Wall loads—Instruct hitters to get into their stance with chests and shoulders facing a padded wall. They should stand close enough to the wall so their fingertips can touch it when their elbows are at their side, with their hands out front. The toes of both feet should create a straight line that is also parallel to the wall. Players create their stance and should practice loading and striding without their hands casting away from the body and touching the wall. No bat is needed.

4. Padded wall swings—This drill is initiated in the same fashion as the previous drill except for the use of a bat and a padded wall to protect the bat from damage. The main difference in setup is that players move just far enough away from the wall for the knob of the bat to be against their navel, and the cap of the bat to touch the wall before creating their stance. The hitter begins the drill with a load

and stride. The second phase is to perform a correct swing without the bat making contact with the padded wall. If the hitter casts, he or she will not be able to perform a swing without hitting the wall.

Flaw #7: Hitching

Description: Once in the batter's stance, the hitter drops his or her hands towards the ground before raising them back up to start the swing.

Problem: Hitching is a wasted motion that can cause serious timing and mechanical problems for a hitter, especially when the pitching speed increases. When a hitter is late getting his or her hands back to a good loading point (at or slightly above the back shoulder in the knockout slot), it creates a poor swing path to the baseball, often causing the hitter to dip the back shoulder and swing up or scoop the baseball **(Figure 5.13)**. This bad habit will cause the hitter to be inconsistent by swinging and missing or hitting too many fly balls.

Goal: The batter should be in the best position to hit every pitch. It's important to remove any body action that increases the chance of failure. The big muscles of the hitter's body should be gathered, and hands of the hitter should be loaded in the knockout slot, ready to attack the ball. The hands should be at or slightly above the level of the back shoulder **(Figure 5.14)**.

FIGURE 5.13

The process of hitching can put the hitter at risk of poorly executing the swing.

FIGURE 5.14

This hitter has kept his hands high, in a good loaded position, so he can work down to hit the baseball.

Drills:

Refer to Player-Pitch (Ages 9–10) "Hitting Drills" on the DVD for the following drills:

1. High tee drill (see "Hitting Drills [C]" on the disc).
2. Double tee drill (see "Hitting Drills [B]" on the disc).

Flaw #8: Front Shoulder Opening Early

Description: In an attempt to swing the bat faster or create more power, the hitter initiates the swing by incorrectly opening and "pulling off" (away) the front shoulder. This motion takes the hitter's front hip, head, and bat barrel out of the hitting zone too early.

Problem: Starting the swing with the front shoulder hinders the hitter from staying behind the ball and recognizing the pitch correctly. This pull-away action of the front shoulder also straightens the front arm, creating a barring out effect (see Flaw #5), which slows down the barrel and causes the bat to prematurely exit the hitting zone. This increases the failure rate. Hitters who pull their front shoulder have trouble consistently hitting the outside strike to the opposite field with any power, and this often creates a hooking effect in their swing **(Figure 5.15)**.

Goal: To keep the front shoulder under control with good direction (towards the pitcher), the hitter wants to start the swing by firing the back hip, back knee, and hands together. To help keep the front side (shoulder, hip, and head) on the ball longer, the stride foot should stay slightly closed (not pointed directly at the pitcher). When the swing starts, the hitter should drive the heel of the stride foot straight down into the ground (in other words, not rotating towards the back foot). This simple process keeps the front side from pulling away from the ball too early **(Figure 5.16)**.

Drills:

Refer to Player-Pitch (Ages 9–10) "Hitting Drills" on the DVD for the following drills:

1. Basic outer third tee drill (see "Hitting Drills [A]" on the disc).
2. Basketball outer third tee drill (see "Hitting Drills [D]" on the disc).

FIGURE 5.15

This hitter has opened his front shoulder early and pulled off the ball in an attempt to swing the bat faster or harder.

FIGURE 5.16

This hitter has kept the front shoulder closed and therefore will be able to stay on the ball and hit it hard to all fields.

Flaw #9: Lazy Bat Barrel

Description: The hitter allows the bat barrel to dip or drop towards the ground as he or she starts the swing to the baseball.

Problem: A lazy barrel will cause the hitter to execute a poor swing plane **(Figure 5.17)**. It also can cause the back shoulder to collapse or break down as the body attempts to adjust to this mechanical flaw in the swing. The result is a long swing with many misses or fly balls.

Goal: Every hitter should keep the barrel of the bat near the body and about shoulder-height, or in between the elbow and the shoulder, as the hands drive the knob of the bat to the baseball **(Figure 5.18)**. This will create "barrel delay" and energy will be effectively stored in the head of the bat. When the hands have arrived near the front hip, the barrel will whip to the ball with the proper angle, and the result will be more consistent solid contact.

FIGURE 5.17

This hitter's barrel has become lazy and dropped too low to create a good swing path to the ball.

FIGURE 5.18

This hitter maintains the correct barrel angle as he takes his hands to the ball.

Drills:

 Refer to Player-Pitch (Ages 9–10) "Hitting Drills" on the DVD for the following drills:

1. Double tee drill (see "Hitting Drills [B]" on the disc).
2. High tee drill (see "Hitting Drills [C]" on the disc).

Flaw #10: Rolling Wrists on Contact (Poor Swing Plane)

Description: The bat barrel gets to the contact point with the baseball and the hitter rolls his or her top hand over the handle of the bat.

Problem: When a hitter rolls his or her wrists before contact with the baseball, it causes the wrists to be in a weak position **(Figure 5.19)**. He or she will probably weakly hit the top part of the ball, causing a "rollover ground ball." Rolling the wrists on contact also prevents the hitter from achieving good extension through the ball. As a result, the bat head will prematurely exit the hitting zone and reduce the chance of consistent solid contact with the ball. Note that a poor grip on the bat can force the hands into a rolled position on contact.

FIGURE 5.19

This hitter rolls his wrist when making contact with the ball, which usually results in a weak hit.

FIGURE 5.20

This hitter creates a strong posture position with palm up/palm down to begin extension through the baseball.

Goal: The hitter should maintain "palm up/palm down" throughout contact and extension to keep the bat head in the hitting zone and on the same plane as long as possible. This provides the greatest chance of solid contact between bat and ball. The hitter should take a short, quick swing to the ball and then attempt to stay long during contact. Hence the teaching cue "short to, long through." It's as if the hitter is trying to hit ten baseballs back to back as opposed to one. Once full extension with balance has been achieved and the hands are in a palm up/palm down position (one hand on the bat faces the sky and the other towards the ground), the hitter then rolls both wrists to finish the swing, which happens well after contact **(Figure 5.20)**.

Drills:

 Refer to Player-Pitch (Ages 9–10) "Hitting Drills [D]" on the DVD for the following drill:

1. Basketball tee drill.

Flaw #11: Poor Extension

Description: The hitter gets the barrel of the bat to the point of contact but removes it prematurely from the hitting zone.

Problem: The hitter will have difficulty making consistent contact because his or her timing has to be perfect to hit the ball solidly. The hitter will also have trouble driving the ball to all parts of the field. The result is an increased failure rate. Poor extension can be caused by a number of hitting flaws including barring out, casting, pulling the shoulder off the ball, and rolling the wrists on contact **(Figure 5.21)**.

Goal: All good hitters should take the barrel of the bat to the baseball with a short, quick swing while maintaining good posture **(Figure 5.22)**. This puts the hitter behind the ball in a palm up/palm down position, allowing the largest window of time for the bat to make solid contact.

FIGURE 5.21

This hitter cuts off his swing by prematurely taking the bat out of the path of the ball, resulting in poor extension.

FIGURE 5.22

This hitter gets good extension of the barrel through contact, which results in a solid hit.

Drills:

Refer to Player-Pitch (Ages 9–10) "Hitting Drills [D]" on the DVD for the first drill:

1. Basketball tee drill.
2. Weight bag drill. A coach or parent can suspend a canvas punching bag from the ceiling by a chain (it is recommended that you use a very light bag for this age group). The player hits the bag with a fundamentally sound swing, making contact and extending, which drives the bag away (back towards the pitcher).

Flaw #12: Poor Backside Rotation

Description: The hitter completes the swing, leaving out the energy from the bottom half of his or her body.

Problem: Becoming a good hitter at all levels of the game requires the use of the whole body. Body parts are linked together and energy is created and transferred from the feet to finish in the barrel of the bat. The strongest muscles of the body are in the legs, buttocks, and hips. If the hitter does not drive the back knee to the ball, which results in the back heel rotating to the sky, the swing will be poor because it is executed with mainly the upper body **(Figure 5.23)**.

Goal: The hitter should use his or her whole body to create a short, quick swing. Good hitters use their lower body and hips in the swing by taking their back knee to the pitched baseball (the back knee will move 6 to 8 inches towards the ball as the back heel rotates to the sky). This allows the hips to fully rotate **(Figure 5.24)**. On the conclusion of the swing, the back leg will finish bent in an "L" position, often referred to as a "power L".

FIGURE 5.23

This hitter fails to use the bottom half of his body because he kept his back foot planted in the clay.

FIGURE 5.24

This hitter transfers the energy created by the legs and hips to the upper body and hands.

Drills:

1. Instruct your players to execute 25 to 30 dry swings, finishing the swing with their back knee to the ball (where contact would have been made) and heel to the sky. Tell them that, at the conclusion of the swing, an imaginary camera mounted on the front of their back knee would be able to take a clear photo of the baseball when it is hit.

2. It does not matter which hitting drill you choose from this book, DVD, or your own list. A hitter should always get backside rotation. Thus, at the conclusion of every swing, ask your hitter to freeze and check for proper back foot position.

CHAPTER 6

PITCHING FLAWS OF NINE- AND TEN-YEAR-OLDS

Myth #1: PITCHING REQUIRES DEVELOPING A SET OF UNIQUE AND COMPLICATED SKILLS. IT IS VERY COMPLEX TO DIAGNOSE AND SOLVE PITCHING FLAWS BECAUSE EACH PLAYER HAS HIS OR HER OWN DIFFICULTIES.

Secret: *Pitching requires fundamentally sound throwing mechanics. Generally, pitching flaws fall into a few different categories and types, but many pitchers at this age exhibit similar weaknesses that you can address.*

Myth #2: PITCHERS SHOULD BE TAUGHT TO THROW CURVEBALLS SO THEY CAN TRICK THE HITTERS AND WIN GAMES FOR THEIR TEAM.

Secret: *Pitchers should not be taught or attempt to throw a curveball even if it helps their team win the Ten and Under National Youth Championship. Incorrectly throwing a curveball can cause serious arm injury that may prematurely curtail a child's playing days. The emphasis should be placed on developing a fundamental delivery with the ability to throw fastballs and changeups.*

Myth #3: ALL PITCHERS SHOULD BE TAUGHT TO THROW IN EXACTLY THE SAME WAY.

Secret: *Contrary to popular belief, there is no one "cookie cutter" way to teach pitching. Just look at Major League players and it won't take long to see that pitchers use their bodies differently to achieve success. However, it is important to keep in mind that there are certain elements or processes that should take place with a fundamentally sound delivery to give a pitcher a chance at achieving long-term success.*

DIAGNOSTICS

Baseball is a very unique game—maybe the only one—in that the defense controls the ball. Because of this, the pitcher is a very important player who has the potential to control or significantly influence the outcome of a game. As a result, there is a lot of pressure put on individual pitchers to do well. If they have a bad game, they will likely cost their team a loss.

In most leagues, players don't start pitching until they are nine years old. If they have progressed through a league that implements a developmentally appropriate system such as the one in this book, players have been working on becoming better throwers since they were in T-ball. It will not be all that difficult for players to transfer those skills to the pitcher's mound. Unfortunately, this is not the case for most players in youth leagues where fundamental throwing mechanics and reinforcement drills are overlooked. As a result, these players may develop poor muscle memory that will likely have to be addressed in the years to come, especially if they attempt to pitch.

At the nine- and ten-year-old age group, coaches and parents often encounter pitchers who have significant flaws with their mechanics. Experienced coaches have tried-and-tested drills that can help get a pitcher back on track. Inexperienced coaches may have a very hard time even diagnosing what is wrong with a pitcher's mechanics. The problem is that there are very few experienced coaches at this level of baseball, and even fewer who understand fundamental pitching mechanics. This puts responsibility to learn back on the coach or parents—the player must be able to count on them to find his or her flaws and provide correct advice on how to fix the problem.

Go to the Video

Videotape your pitchers so you can go back and watch the video in slow motion or frame-by-frame to locate flaws based on correct pitching mechanics for the player's age (as presented in the accompanying DVD). Like all other athletes, pitchers are creatures of habit. Unless they are shown otherwise, many pitchers are convinced they are performing the phases of a pitching delivery correctly, even if they aren't. Video analysis is a great tool for coaches to capture and demonstrate a pitcher's mechanical flaws.

Because a pitcher's arm and hand can reach high speeds in a fraction of a second, it often takes slowing down the process to successfully diagnose problems. Watching the video frame-by-frame can help a coach, player, or parent determine whether the pitcher's body parts are consistently getting to the right places at the right times within the delivery. It is best to analyze video from the side and front views of the pitcher.

Once the problems are diagnosed, correct or adjust only one weakness at a time so you don't overwhelm a pitcher. A player can use a full-length mirror to repeatedly reinforce the proper movement sequence ("dry mechanics") within the delivery they are focusing on. Once one weakness is fixed, move to the next weakness that needs to be addressed. Start with big problems and work toward smaller issues with the pitcher's mechanics. The goal is to establish mechanics that help support good control, velocity, and, most importantly, arm care.

How to Analyze a Pitcher on Video

Use this sequence to analyze the video of a pitcher you are trying to diagnose:

- Hold a sheet of paper over the screen, cover everything except the lower half of the pitcher's body, and look for flaws.
- Cover the legs and watch the middle torso/hips for flaws.
- Cover the pitcher from the waist down and observe the head/shoulders for flaws.
- Study the action of both arms from start to finish.
- Lastly, study whole body mechanics from start to finish.

The Miracle Drill?

Don't get caught up trying to find or implement a "miracle pitching drill" that is full of "wow power." Pitching drills that are fancy, complicated, not appropriate for young pitchers, or attempt to work on many parts of the delivery at once can cause problems instead of fixing them. Good coaches know that simple, tried-and-tested drills are usually the best to address a particular weakness.

Apply Skills to the Game

Drills are worthless if a pitcher does not make the connection from the "lab" (bullpen or side mounds) to the actual pitcher's mound. Most pitchers have the initial tendency to revert to previous delivery mechanics when they see a hitter step into the batter's box. To cure this, create a game environment in practice or provide game-like stress on the pitcher whenever possible in drill work.

THE TWELVE COMMON PITCHING FLAWS

Following are twelve common flaws found at the beginning level of pitching, which is usually the nine- and ten-year-old age group. If you are a coach or parent, take time to go through the pitching mechanics as listed in Chapter 3 and familiarize yourself with the skill sequence photos. Then take time to review the pitching mechanics and drills on the accompanying DVD. This will help you digest the following flaws and understand the drills to address them. Continue to implement and emphasize proper throwing mechanics and drills at the start of every practice, which will also help your pitchers improve.

Flaw #1: Improper Grip of the Ball

Description: The player incorrectly grips the baseball while delivering a pitch to the plate.

Problem: An improper grip on the ball is the most fundamental problem a pitcher can have. It will cause difficulty with the pitcher's accuracy and a loss of velocity. Many young pitchers "choke" the baseball by holding it deep in their palm and squeezing it too tightly **(Figure 6.1)**.

Goal: The pitcher should use a relaxed grip, with two fingers on top of the baseball. As the player matures and his or her hand grows, the ball should be kept away from the palm (except when throwing a changeup). The thumb should be underneath the ball and in a position close to splitting the distance between the top two fingers **(Figure 6.2)**. Pitchers this age should be taught a four-seam fastball grip (across the "horseshoe" that is created by the shape of the laces), a two-seam fastball grip, and a changeup grip. Please see details on the specific pitching grips taught in Chapter 3.

Drills:

1. Line up your pitchers and give each of them a ball. Ask them to hold out the baseball as you walk along the line and check to ensure they have a correct grip. Make adjustments to each player's grip as needed.

2. After teaching a four-seam grip, two-seam grip, and a changeup, ask your pitchers to hold out the ball and demonstrate that they have mastered each grip. Make adjustments as necessary.

FIGURE 6.1

This pitcher is improperly gripping the baseball by holding it deep in his hand and squeezing much too hard.

FIGURE 6.2

This pitcher is correctly gripping the ball, holding it relaxed, so his muscles can react quickly to release it.

3. Watch the pitchers in practice to see how they are holding the baseball. Periodically check them by stopping them in motion and asking them to immediately show you their grip of the ball.

4. Players who also are pitchers should alternate their grips when executing general throwing drills and throwing long. This will give them a better feel for the pitches and how the ball reacts when leaving their hand. Encourage pitchers to tweak their two-seam and changeup grips to see if they can achieve more movement or "run" of the ball, which can more easily deceive hitters.

Flaw #2: Maximum Effort

Description: A pitcher exerts 100 percent effort attempting to throw the ball as hard as possible.

Problem: A pitcher who throws with 100 percent effort, or "maximum effort," will, in fact, not throw the ball any harder, but will lose considerable command (ability to locate the pitches). Pitchers who exert maximum effort not only subject themselves to control problems, but increased arm injuries, excess soreness, and longer recovery periods. This is a result of tightening the different muscles of the body when trying to generate more power (**Figure 6.3**).

FIGURE 6.3

This pitcher is throwing with 100 percent effort; even the muscles in his neck and face have tightened in an attempt to throw the ball harder.

FIGURE 6.4

This player is delivering a pitch with 90 percent effort, which will improve his chances of throwing more strikes and reduce the stress on his arm and body.

Goal: A pitcher should strive to achieve maximum fastball velocity by using only 90 percent of his or her maximum physical effort. Ninety percent effort means the pitcher will not strain or tighten up to throw **(Figure 6.4)**. Tight muscles are slow muscles that don't perform well.

Drills:

1. Demonstrate to pitchers that 90 percent effort is equal to 100 percent velocity and command. If you have access to a radar gun, track pitches in the bullpen and ask pitchers to muscle up to 100 percent effort for a couple pitches. Make note of the velocity and accuracy of the pitch. Then ask the pitcher to relax and deliver a few pitches at 90 percent and make note of velocity and accuracy. Proof is in the results.

2. Show pitchers that the location of a fastball is more important than the speed of the ball. Teach the concept of "soft contact." The goal is to reduce the number of pitches thrown by making batters hit the pitch softly to the defense, creating easy outs. This saves the arm

of the pitcher and takes away the feeling that the pitcher has to be perfect to win and strike everyone out.

Flaw #3: Using Less than the Whole Body to Pitch

Description: The pitcher neglects to tie the energy created by his or her legs and hips into the delivery of the pitch.

Problem: When a pitcher fails to channel the energy created by his or her legs and hips into the delivery of the pitch, it puts a large amount of stress on the shoulder and elbow **(Figure 6.5)**. The pitcher will also tire easily and usually suffer prolonged shoulder and elbow soreness or increased chances for injury in the pitching arm.

Goal: Every pitcher should tap into or use all the energy created by the legs and rotation of the hips to reduce the stress on the shoulder and elbow when throwing a pitch **(Figure 6.6)**.

FIGURE **6.5**

This pitcher is throwing with his arm only and not harnessing energy from his legs and hips.

FIGURE **6.6**

This pitcher is effectively using his body to stay connected and transfer the energy from his legs through his hips and torso into his shoulders and, ultimately, into the ball.

Drills:

1. Dry mechanics—Ask your pitchers to go through the phases of the delivery without a ball. Watch them carefully and videotape them to see if they are incorporating sound mechanics into the pitch. Look for throwing flaws that can let stored energy escape the delivery without being effectively used.

2. General throwing drills—Be sure to implement all the basic throwing drills into your official practices and at home. Throwing drills that are used for all positions teach players to use their whole body.

Flaw #4: Inconsistent Balance

Description: The pitcher fails to create consistent dynamic balance (balance points) before delivering the pitch to the plate.

Problem: When a pitcher has poor dynamic balance within their mechanics, problems with pitch delivery will result, including the inability to consistently control the pitch and increased failure rates **(Figure 6.7)**.

Goal: All pitchers should create dynamic balance in their delivery. This goes from low balance, as the pitcher lifts the front leg, into high balance, where the front knee reaches its highest point before it descends to the plate. It is important that a pitcher gathers his or her energy to a consistent balance point. The pitcher's head should be aligned with the navel and his or her weight controlled vertically over the back leg (the leg furthest from the plate) before starting the directional phase of the delivery **(Figure 6.8)**. If a player's weight is in a different place on every pitch, it will be difficult to consistently repeat the delivery, which is vital to becoming an effective pitcher.

Drills:

 Refer to Player-pitch (Ages 9–10) "Pitching Drills" on the DVD for the first three drills:

1. Coach hand-off drill (see "Pitching Drills [A]" on the disc).
2. Coach toss balance drill (see "Pitching Drills [B]" on the disc).
3. Bucket drill (see "Pitching Drills [D]" on the disc).

FIGURE 6.7

This pitcher shows poor balance because he is leaning backwards. This will make it difficult to consistently throw strikes.

FIGURE 6.8

This pitcher is using dynamic balance to create a consistent position to start his delivery to the plate.

4. Balance drill—Coaches command their pitchers to lift their front knee to the highest point of their leg lift and hold for a count of 5 seconds. Then they can work up to 10 seconds.

Flaw #5: Poor Direction of the Landing (Stride) Foot

Description: The pitcher delivers the pitch, but the stride (front) foot does not land in line with the back foot, pointed directly to home plate. The stride foot ends up landing too closed (for a right-handed pitcher, the foot lands on the third base side of the imaginary line to the plate) or too open (for a right-handed pitcher, the foot lands on the first base side of the imaginary line to the plate).

Problem: If the foot lands closed to the plate, the body will not be able to effectively "link" the energy created in the delivery. The body will lock and then have to rotate around itself causing the pitcher to have difficulty with location or control **(Figure 6.9)**. If the front foot lands open, the hips will open prematurely in the delivery of the pitch, and the pitcher will lose the ability to effectively explode the hips into the pitch. This will diminish accuracy. This movement puts extra stress on the elbow and shoulder because the pitcher's shoulder has to bear more load due to the loss of energy of the hips.

FIGURE **6.9**

This pitcher is landing closed with the stride foot, thus the body works against itself in an attempt to deliver the pitch.

FIGURE **6.10**

This pitcher creates good direction to the plate by landing on the imaginary "T" created with the pitcher's rubber and the front foot.

Goal: Every pitcher should land with the stride (front) foot pointed straight at the plate **(Figure 6.10)**. An imaginary straight line should be drawn from the ball of the back foot (which is set parallel to the pitcher's rubber) and end up at home plate. This straight line is where the stride foot should land as it plants into the ground. This creates good direction to the plate, which is needed for consistent location or control.

Drills:

 Refer to Player-Pitch (Ages 9–10) "Pitching Drills [E]" on the DVD for the following drill:

1. T-drill (not to be confused with the hitting tee drill).

Flaw #6: Poor Use of the Front Arm in the Delivery

Description: On delivery of the pitch, the player's glove arm pulls away from the target (plate).

Problem: Poor front-arm action causes momentum and direction problems with the delivery of the pitch. If the pitcher's glove moves away from the target too early, it will pull his or her front shoulder and head out of line causing directional or control problems **(Figure 6.11)**. If the pitcher fails to tap into the energy created by effectively using the front arm and glove, he or she will put more stress on the throwing arm to compensate for the loss of energy. The pitcher should also avoid aggressively pulling the glove-side elbow into his or her body. This glove-side elbow should move naturally to counter the movement of the throwing arm, creating torque.

Goal: The pitcher's glove should swivel or rotate in front of his or her body, and the pitcher's chest should move towards the glove during the delivery of the pitch to keep the body in a straight line with home plate **(Figure 6.12)**. Once the throwing hand starts to release the ball to the plate, the glove will naturally move to the side of the ribs as the elbow slides past the hip in a reverse movement of the throwing arm.

FIGURE 6.11

This pitcher is not effectively using his front arm in the delivery. This will cause problems with direction and consistency.

FIGURE 6.12

This pitcher is effectively using his glove side to help create torque and direction to the plate.

Drills:

1. Dry mechanics—Direct the pitchers to go through the phases of the delivery without a ball. Watch them carefully and film them to see if they are incorporating a correct glove-side action into the pitch.

2. Throwing drills—Be sure to implement all the basic general throwing drills for all positions into your official practices and at home. They will teach the pitchers to use their whole body, including their glove side.

3. Weighted glove drill—Place a weighted object, such as a one-pound to three-pound weight, in the pitcher's glove. Smaller players can use lighter weights and even remove the glove and hold it in their bare hand. As players perform throwing drills or pitches from the mound, they can feel how the body works as a whole to throw because the weight must move from the front of the body to a position close to the side of the ribs to create torque needed for the throwing arm. If pitchers take the weight away from the body or move it too low towards the thigh, it immediately lets them know they are performing the movement incorrectly.

Flaw #7: Pushing or Cutting the Pitch

Description: The pitcher's throwing hand moves to a position under or to the side of the ball on release, and this causes a push or cut of the pitch. Pushing is often the result of lack of arm strength and a compensation to get the ball to the plate. Cutting the hand to the side of the ball is usually a problem with throwing mechanics.

Problem: Pushing the baseball upon delivery of the pitch will result in a significant loss of velocity. The pitcher will also create other flaws in the delivery by compensating with the body and arm for this incorrect release of the pitch **(Figure 6.13)**. A pitcher who cuts the ball by moving his or her hand to the side of the baseball on release also loses velocity and the ability to control the ball. Both issues result in increased failure rates. This hand position will also make it difficult to effectively learn and use secondary pitches such as a changeup.

Goal: Every pitcher in ten-and-under baseball should be taught to keep two throwing fingers on top of the ball, and also to keep the pitching

FIGURE 6.13

This pitcher is pushing the ball to the plate by allowing his hand to slide underneath the ball at release.

FIGURE 6.14

This pitcher is staying on top of and behind the baseball, which will create a more consistent and effective release of the ball.

hand behind the ball to create the ability to pitch "downhill." This allows the pitcher to create a consistent release point with solid mechanics **(Figure 6.14)**.

Drills:

 Refer to T-Ball (Ages 4–6) "Throwing Drills" on the DVD for the following drill:

1. Wrist flip drill.

Flaw #8: Jumping at the Catcher

Description: In an attempt to throw the ball forcefully, the pitcher pushes so hard off the pitcher's rubber that he or she appears to jump at the plate.

Problem: Jumping or pushing too hard off the pitcher's rubber will result in the front side (front foot, hip, and shoulder) rushing open too early, and

FIGURE **6.15**

This player is jumping at the plate to deliver the pitch, which can cause many inconsistencies in the release of the ball.

FIGURE **6.16**

This pitcher is implementing a controlled lateral movement to the plate that effectively uses his hips to create increased arm speed.

it leaves the throwing arm fighting to catch up with the body **(Figure 6.15)**. This puts undue stress on the throwing elbow and shoulder and also results in a very large stride. If not corrected, pitchers who jump at the plate usually have difficulty throwing a consistent secondary pitch, such as a changeup or, down the road, a curveball.

Goal: Every pitcher should create a controlled lateral movement to the plate by storing energy in his or her high balance point. The pitcher wants to lead with the outside front heel to the plate to keep the hips closed as long as possible. Then he or she should push off the rubber just before the front foot lands to explode the pelvis into rotation to increase arm speed **(Figure 6.16)**.

Drills:

 Refer to Player-Pitch (Ages 9–10) "Pitching Drills [D]" on the DVD for the following drill:

1. Bucket drill.

Flaw 9: Tilting the Body and Head on the Pitch

Description: As the pitch is released, the pitcher's head and shoulders tilt diagonally and fall out of body alignment, creating bad posture.

Problem: This incorrect movement of the upper body causes alignment, balance, and posture problems, which ultimately result in control problems. Often this action is the result of trying to overthrow the pitch **(Figure 6.17)**.

Goal: Every pitcher should try to maintain good posture throughout the delivery. This means maintaining alignment and dynamic balance by keeping the head centered over the navel until the controlled lateral movement to the plate begins. At that point, the chin points straight to the plate with the shoulders square (parallel to the ground)—they do not tilt diagonally. As the pitcher releases the ball, his or her head, front shoulder, glove, and front knee should be in a line with the catcher's glove, with the shoulders remaining square. The head should finish directly over or just past the front knee **(Figure 6.18)**.

FIGURE 6.17

This pitcher has created a poor balance and posture problem by tilting the shoulders on the release of the ball to the plate.

FIGURE 6.18

This player is using fundamental pitching mechanics by maintaining good shoulder alignment (parallel to the ground).

Drills:

1. Dry pitching mechanics—Ask the pitcher to freeze in the power position and then move slowly into the release point. Make sure the shoulders stay parallel to the ground.

2. Place a mirror about ten feet in front of the pitcher. Complete dry pitching mechanics and see if the pitcher can keep his or her eyes and shoulders parallel to the ground while pointing the chin directly to the target.

3. Throwing drills—Be sure to implement all the basic throwing drills in your official practices and at home. These teach pitchers how to correctly align the body to throw.

Flaw #10: Inconsistent Arm Slot (Release Point)

Description: The pitcher releases the baseball from a different or inconsistent location on every pitch.

Problem: Throwing a baseball requires a complex combination of the body's large and small muscle groups working together in precise timing to produce a specific result. Pitchers who don't have a consistent release point continually adjust to releasing the baseball at different heights and locations in relation to the body **(Figure 6.19)**. This makes it very difficult for a pitcher to throw consistent strikes. Some pitchers throw their fastball from one arm slot (the release point of the pitch) and their secondary pitch, such as a changeup, from another arm slot. As pitchers advance up the ladder of baseball to higher levels, using different arm slots for different pitches telegraphs to the hitter which pitch is being thrown, removing the element of deception.

Goal: A pitcher should create a correct delivery, essentially replicating the same mechanics on every pitch he or she throws **(Figure 6.20)**. A consistent arm slot or release point will give the pitcher the greatest chance for an element of unpredictability to the hitter. As a pitcher improves over time, he or she will eventually desire to have pinpoint control to any part of the strike zone.

Drills:

1. Videotape the pitcher from in front or behind, using a tripod for the camera. Ask the pitcher to throw a fastball and changeup, and review the video to see if the arm slot is noticeably different.

FIGURE 6.19

This photo depicts a pitcher using different arm slots to deliver the ball to the plate, causing inconsistencies and control problems.

FIGURE 6.20

This pitcher utilizes a consistent release point with his elbow near shoulder level, working "downhill" to the plate.

2. Throwing drills—Be sure to implement all the basic throwing drills in your official practices and at home. These will help pitchers implement a consistent arm slot.

Flaw #11: Not Loading the Hips to Pitch (Pelvic Loading)

Description: The pitcher raises his or her front leg, bringing it to the high balance point position, but fails to bring the front knee close enough to the center line of the body, which will adequately load the hips for the pitch.

Problem: When a pitcher fails to adequately load his or her hips, energy is lost in the hip rotation phase of the pitch delivery. This puts more strain on the arm and shoulder to make up for the lost energy. It also slows the rotation of the arm, which decreases arm speed **(Figure 6.21)**.

Goal: A pitcher can create more velocity by increasing hip speed during delivery of the pitch. Hip speed directly relates to arm speed. When the pitcher reaches the highest point in the front knee lift, that knee should be closer to the center line of the body than it is to the front foot, when viewed from the side **(Figure 6.22)**. This slight inward turn of the front

FIGURE 6.21

This pitcher fails to load his hips in the delivery of the pitch, which decreases arm speed and puts more stress on the shoulder and elbow.

FIGURE 6.22

This pitcher is effectively loading his hips, which will allow energy to be stored and increase hip rotation speed. This will increase arm speed.

knee loads the hips or pelvis. This loading process for a pitcher is similar to what hitters are trying to do when they get their load to store energy and release it effectively into the swing.

Drills:

 Refer to Player-pitch (Ages 9–10) "Pitching Drills [D]" on the DVD for the following drill:

1. Bucket drill.

Flaw #12: Bending the Back Incorrectly

Description: A pitcher completes the delivery but never reaches a point after the release of the baseball when his or her back is close to parallel to the ground. In other words, the pitcher stays erect through the entire delivery of the pitch.

Problem: If a pitcher does not bend his or her back through the delivery, he or she is not effectively creating direction towards the plate. In addition the pitcher is failing to maximize velocity and command of the pitch **(Figure 6.23)**.

Goal: A pitcher wants to direct his or her chin towards the catcher's glove, and the pitcher's head should finish out over the front (landing) knee at about the time the ball is released from the throwing hand. This action causes the back to bend. After release, the throwing arm should naturally finish outside and very close to the pitcher's landing knee **(Figure 6.24)**.

Drills:

 Refer to Player-pitch (Ages 9–10) "Pitching Drills [C]" on the DVD for the following drill:

1. Towel drill.

FIGURE 6.23

This pitcher is not creating effective direction to the plate because he is standing straight up.

FIGURE 6.24

This pitcher is creating good direction to the plate by taking his chin to the catcher's mitt as he delivers the pitch. This results in a flat back that is close to parallel to the ground.

CHAPTER 7

THE STATE OF YOUTH BASEBALL

Myth #1: PARENTS IN THE UNITED STATES HAVE A GOOD PERSPECTIVE ON YOUTH BASEBALL.

Secret: *Many parents in the United States have significantly lost perspective on youth baseball and it seems to be a trend that is growing worse every year.*

Myth #2: AT YOUTH BASEBALL GAMES, YOU FIND PARENTS RELAXING IN THEIR CHAIRS, ENJOYING THE GAME, AND CHEERING ON ALL PLAYERS TO DO THEIR BEST.

Secret: *Many of today's youth baseball parents have become very selfish. They only concern themselves with their own child. Unfortunately, this selfish way of thinking is often passed down to the child.*

Myth #3: THE MORE PARENTS PUSH THEIR CHILD TO FOCUS ON BASEBALL AND IMPROVING THEIR SKILL LEVEL, THE MORE LIKELY IT IS THAT HE OR SHE WILL EVENTUALLY RECEIVE A COLLEGE SCHOLARSHIP OR GET DRAFTED INTO MAJOR LEAGUE BASEBALL.

Secret: *Baseball, at all amateur levels and especially at the youth level, should be played for fun. Goals of lucrative scholarships and professional contracts should never be a reason to push a child into playing or specializing in baseball. Of the approximately three million kids in the world playing youth baseball, only about 1,500 will ever receive a college scholarship or get drafted into professional baseball. That means that most players who put on a baseball uniform will one day be doing something other than playing for an education and even fewer will be playing for a living.*

WHERE ARE WE HEADING?

Two things are certain: we love our children dearly, and there are no perfect parents. We each have our own strengths and weaknesses. That is what makes the world go 'round. The problem is that parents are rapidly losing their perspective on how their child fits into youth baseball, and this is sending the wrong messages and teaching the wrong lessons to the children. Not all parents are negative. There are still a percentage of adults who keep youth baseball in perspective. However, this is a growing problem that needs to be addressed. I want to apologize up front for the strong statements I feel I must make to shed light on this concern. If I sugarcoat the issues or skirt around the problems to keep from hurting people's feelings then I have failed to tell the truth. This will only slow the healing process that is so desperately needed on America's ballfields.

I have personally witnessed a major shift in the negative influence parents can have on their child and the inappropriate involvement of parents with coaches. Parental issues and problems develop when the players are young, and they seem to grow and escalate by the time the child is in high school. It is my sincere hope that parents will take to heart the problems discussed on the following pages and do everything in their power to be an agent for positive change.

Generally, the youth baseball parents who need to read this section of the book the most are usually those who don't think they have a problem. Thus, if you are a baseball parent reading this chapter, you probably are trying to educate yourself on the disturbing trends and negative behaviors of parents of this generation so you can avoid these common pitfalls. Please understand that, as hard as it may be to believe that grown mothers and fathers behave in the ways outlined in this chapter, in many instances the situations are worse. I could write a separate book on parental ethics at the high school level that would leave you shaking your head in utter disbelief. In fact, many parents are unknowingly destroying their children's baseball experience, and this is happening at every level of the game, including T-ball (four-, five-, and six-year-olds).

Just like a player who is a bad influence on his or her team, it just takes a few bad parents to make the baseball experience miserable for everyone inside and outside the fence. Parents regularly demonstrate poor behavior, such as yelling and screaming at umpires, barking instructions to their child, questioning decisions the coach makes, scrutinizing their child's performance, making insensitive comments to those around them, and acting as though each game their child plays is the seventh game of the World Series. They will quickly have an out-of-body experience if their child is not playing as much as they think he or she should be, or is not playing the position they think is the right one! You would think the whole world is coming to an end over one youth baseball game.

The problem is that baseball is a difficult game to play successfully due to the hand-eye coordination and fine motor abilities that are needed. Baseball is an even harder game to teach properly; the fundamental strategies of the game become progressively more complex as the skill level and strength of the players improve. There are usually many decisions made by coaches that benefit the whole team, but some of these may not seem logical to the parent who has only the best interest of his or her own child in mind.

Parents watching youth baseball should be concerned that the players have fun, learn fundamentals, and develop teamwork skills, but don't try to convince many youth baseball parents of that. They believe their child is going to earn a college scholarship in baseball or be the next Major League superstar. It's fine to have expectations for one's child, but pushing expectations that are nearly impossible to meet ultimately leaves the child feeling like a failure!

No Exemption

There does not seem to be an amateur baseball team in America that is exempt from overzealous or obnoxious parents. Each time I speak with peers in the coaching profession, no matter what state in the nation or what age players they are working with, the first thing that comes up in conversation is that parents are making it much harder to enjoy coaching the kids. For instance, there is now a youth baseball complex in South Carolina that only allows parents to sit in the bleachers behind the outfield fence. This was done so players will be far enough away from their parents to listen to their coach and have fun. If that does not send a wake-up call to the parents, I don't know what will. Can the situation improve? I believe it will. However, we must first admit that it is a huge problem and get the issues out on the table. George Whitfield, North Carolina Baseball Hall of Fame inductee, states: "Parents need to let their child play the game and have fun. Too many parents try to live through their children and it does nothing but hurt them. Sometimes they just need to sit back and enjoy the game with their mouth closed. They must begin to realize that they are looking out for one player (their child) and the coach is looking out for the whole team."

Rose-Colored Glasses

Another example of parents becoming an obstacle for their child's success when it comes to baseball performance can be witnessed in the rose-colored glasses that many adults allow themselves to wear. They often make the dangerous mistake of sharing their unrealistic perceptions of their child's ability level with the child. Parents regularly overestimate the skills and abilities of their children. This process sets up the kids for failure because they will eventually believe what their parents think. Like the parents, the children become self-absorbed, and they are quick to point fingers or make excuses when things don't go their way. As a result, the parents have created a "me" player who tends to be a negative thinker. Players like this will likely spend their years in baseball feeling they are being mistreated when they don't win the position that their parents think they ought to play, bat at the top of the batting order, win a spot in the starting lineup, or one day secure a college scholarship. Instead of being the team players they should be, negative players will spread their thinking throughout the team, infecting it like a virus from the inside out. It only takes one of these players to quickly infect their whole team and ruin a whole baseball season for all involved.

The Rise in Violence

If you have not been at a youth baseball game recently, take a leisurely stroll to the ballpark this spring or summer. But wait, you'd better bring earplugs. Boxing gloves might not be a bad idea either. Statistics tell us there is a good chance you will come across some wild and crazy parents who will be yelling and screaming at everyone, including the players, coaches, and umpires. There is even a good chance that you will witness a verbal or physical fight between parents, a parent and a coach, a parent and the umpire, or a parent and his child! You may have heard the old adage, "I went to a fight and a hockey game broke out." Well, before long, the saying may change to, "I went to a fight and a youth baseball game broke out." It is truly getting that ridiculous.

What messages are we sending to our kids? Parents are living and dying with each at-bat their child has. Do you think the kids can't feel the pressure they're under to perform? Add to it the recent trend to start all-star teams as early as T-ball, and the circus begins.

This issue of violence is complex because it is tied to strong emotions. If parents get emotionally caught up in their child's game, they quickly become like an angry swarm of bees. Some youth baseball organizations across the country are beginning to require parents of participants to sign "sportsmanship contracts" that state they will conduct themselves in sportsmanlike manner while at the ballpark. In order to get a grip on this problem, or even slow down this alarming trend, parents are going to have to make a conscious effort to put youth baseball back into perspective. When that happens, emotions will calm and the tempers will defuse.

WHO IS PLAYING?

No one wants to be accused of living vicariously through his or her children. Unfortunately, a large number of today's youth baseball parents are doing exactly that. As adults grow older, they begin to realize the opportunities they may have missed or thrown away. Maybe these resulted from bad choices or a relationship that stole that chance to do or be something special. Whatever the case may be, parents don't want their children to make the same mistakes they did. The cycle starts when parents lead their children into experiences they wanted for themselves.

As the child's ability and talents increase, the parent starts to feel good about the attention this commands. Like a drug, the parent seeks and craves more attention through the child. The parent starts to feel every emotion for the child. It's as if what happens to the child is happening to them. The parent gets angry if a call goes against his or her son or daughter. They are envious when another player (and, by association, that player's parents) has a good game and "steals" the attention from their child (and themselves). At higher levels, when players start to get their names in the paper, it makes the parent feel special to have a child who is performing so well and getting noticed. It's as if the parent's own name was typed across the page.

This problem with parents is also very hard to control because it directly ties into their own self-worth and self-confidence (or lack thereof). In order to stop living through their children, parents must understand and be comfortable with the fact that it is not a direct reflection on them whether their child can throw or hit a baseball better than someone else's child. They should encourage and love their children regardless of performance levels. They will be happy with any positive choice their children

are not happy with the position they are asked to play! Many kids have been ingrained with the "me" syndrome from playing on teams that may have been put together to allow them to play the position they or their parents want. If the coach can't then play them in the desired position, the coach must be bad.

If kept in the proper perspective and not overdone, travel baseball teams can provide a great experience for players to compete and improve. Coaches all want their players "game tough" from facing good competition. The problem again lies with the parents who are increasingly losing perspective on what youth baseball is all about. They eventually get sucked into the parental frenzy that is all around them every day at youth ballparks across our nation. A parent who has fallen victim to this way of thinking is a nightmare for a coach to deal with. As a result, it is nearly impossible for players to buy into the team concept emphasized by their coach.

POLITICS IN YOUTH BASEBALL

A coach or parent can't have a discussion about a baseball team or player without the word "politics" being used as some type of excuse for why something is or is not happening. Baseball has the potential to be destroyed by controlling, influential people in the community. This is because of the nature of the game itself, including the way playing time is determined and teams are selected. Some baseball teams require a lot of money for equipment, access to facilities to practice, and tournament entry fees. Parents with ulterior motives and money may try to influence a coach to specifically benefit their own child. It takes a coach with integrity to battle these negative influences, which surround most teams at the youth level. There are three types of politics that must be understood to overcome this perceived obstacle that brings out the worst in parents' behavior.

Real Politics

Real politics are by far the worst type of politics and they are visible almost everywhere in amateur baseball. Parents run the leagues their kids play in. They coach the teams their children play on. They also choose and coach the all-star teams that are made up of the so-called "best players" in the league. Gone are the days when citizens from the community coached teams for the fun of it. Except for a few remaining "die-hards," most youth teams are coached by parents. Thus, parents of the players choose teams, make lineups, and select all-star players. Important variables such as skill level and attitude should be key factors for selection of players, but these are often put at the bottom of the list or left out of the equation completely.

Many coaches at the youth level are mistakenly obsessed with winning and will do anything necessary to ensure victory. They may attempt to "stack" their team (load a team with talented players) by appointing assistant coaches whose children will then automatically qualify for their team. They manipulate the league draft, cheat, and even lie to get the best team. Positions that are "most desirable" on the team are saved for their own child. The coach then nominates their own kid for the all-star team, whether or not he or she deserves it. This type of selfish behavior has been present, to some degree, in amateur baseball for a long time; however, it has become much more evident in recent years. It is obvious that many youth coaches are only in it for their children's personal benefit.

Angry or complaining parents who challenge every decision that a coach makes can negatively influence some coaches who otherwise have a good heart and good intentions. Since many youth baseball coaches are not experienced and may be coaching just so the team can exist, they fall prey to parents who put the most pressure on them. The politics can become more intense when large amounts of money are needed for teams, such as travel teams, to function successfully. Money can quickly destroy the integrity of a team. For example, talented players who may be from homes that can't afford to support their participation on a travel team are sometimes passed over for players whose parents have more money.

Perceived Politics

The second type of politics is perceived politics—the politics don't really exist except in the mind of the parent. This is where parents are really missing the boat. Parents in today's culture are apt to blame someone other than their children for the lack of playing time, not playing a preferred position, or not being chosen for the team. Their child might play for a coach who runs a first-class ball club, has integrity, and plays the best players, but that does not matter to the parent.

If things don't go well for their child, parents will very quickly cry "politics." Coaches have been falsely accused of playing the kids whose parents have the most money, playing all the poor kids, playing kids because they are a minority, not playing kids due to racism, playing kids because they are the coach's favorite, playing kids because . . . you fill in the blank! It's ridiculous. The fact is that most coaches and players ages nine and up enjoy winning (the older the age group, the more fun winning becomes)! Each game has a winner and a loser, and teams probably won't win as many games as they should if their coaches are playing kids for reasons other than talent.

Unfortunately in youth baseball, perceived politics is just as damaging as real politics. It is not uncommon for today's parents to cry "politics" when there are none involved. The problem with parents accusing a coach of playing politics is that he or she will grow tired of hearing excuses from angry parents and stop coaching.

Coaches at the higher levels have not changed that much over the years. They prepare for games, try to teach skills, and put the best players in a role to help the team win. Thus, parents have to start dealing with the reality of *amateur* baseball. Players develop roles based on their strengths and weaknesses and the depth of the talent on the team. Coaches have a responsibility to do what is best for the team, not what is best for one child. Once parents can put things in perspective, they can sit back, relax, and watch their kids have fun playing or being a part of a team!

Valuable Lessons to Be Learned

In recreational baseball, parents pay for their child to be part of a team. Therefore, their child may be entitled to play a specified amount of innings or at bats per game. However, when did the concept evolve that everyone gets a trophy for participating on a youth team? Where in "real life" does everyone get rewarded just for participating in something? Somewhere along the line, someone decided that playing on the team was not good enough anymore. Someone felt that adults were hurting the feelings of the kids (and their parents) who did not get recognized as one of the top players. So one or two angry parents, whose child didn't get a trophy, made a stink, and the rest is history.

Baseball is supposed to teach life lessons, such as "life is not fair." So why do people go to such lengths to spare someone's feelings by giving everyone a trophy when a certificate of participation would suffice? This sends a false message to a kid that says, "no matter what you do, or how good you do it, you will be rewarded anyway." Is this what we want our children to learn in baseball? Other lessons taught and learned through participation in baseball include the dynamics of being a part of a team, and how to deal appropriately with failure and find positive ways to cope with disappointment. Kids learn that some are better than others at sports: if they love to play baseball but are not very good for their age, they have to work harder than the other kids or find something else to play. If these lessons can be effectively taught and learned, that is the real reward for being a part of a baseball team.

Try not to make up excuses for your child when he or she truly is not a top player. The fact that you love your children and support them in all their endeavors, regardless of how well they do, will mean much more than any trophy or award that will eventually collect dust on a shelf and be tucked away in a box.

COMMONSENSE SOLUTIONS

Now that we've explored some of the negative issues surrounding youth baseball, let's look at some simple solutions. This short section will provide a list of ten commonsense steps parents can take to make the game more enjoyable for all involved and help keep a healthy perspective on the game. First, it is important to remember that most coaches at the youth level are parents themselves. They have families, jobs, and other responsibilities that need their time and attention. There are many instances where fathers and mothers take on coaching out of necessity to keep a team going. They are doing the job because no one else will. You will also find that, as easy as it is to know the right thing to do, it is another thing to actually do it. Human emotions can ruin the best of intentions.

1. Spend time practicing at home with your child. This is the single greatest thing you can do to help your child improve. Don't spend time telling them how great they are or how they are being done wrong by the coach. Instead, offer them attention and encourage them to give their best effort. Work on the child's individual weaknesses, but most importantly spend time with him or her, period. Talk positively about the coach, the team, and having fun. Once the games begin, don't coach your child through the fence. And never degrade his or her performance. This is the worst possible thing you can do to embarrass yourself and your child.

2. Ask the coach if you can help run a station at practice. Youth coaches are often overwhelmed. They want to do a good job, but they may not have the knowledge to run an effective practice or to properly teach fundamentals. Practices are much more productive

when there are at least three coaches or parents running specific skill stations for the players. Prepare ahead of time by asking the coach to tell you what you can do at practice so you can prepare one or two effective drills and teach the skill correctly.

3. Ask the coach if you can help keep organization in the dugout. Most youth teams need a dugout dad or mom to keep order while the coach is handling the game. These parents make sure the players know when they are due up to hit, help them find their gloves and hats for defense, and keep players from getting distracted by each other and focused on the game. This person may keep an official score book, and help the coach keep track of innings children have played and who must still get in the game to fulfill league rules.

4. Avoid making any negative comments at games or practices. Simply bite your tongue, swallow your pride, whatever it takes to set a good example for the kids and other parents. This is especially necessary when things are not going well for your team or child. Always speak positively about the team and coach in front of your child. This affirms that you believe in the coach, and it is the job of the players to play and the coach to coach. If you feel you could do a better job, then volunteer to be a coach next season.

5. Avoid negative parents and don't lend them an ear. Disassociate yourself from any negative sources at the ballpark because negative people try to influence other parents. This may even mean sitting away from others if you can't find anyone positive to sit with. Cheer genuinely for everyone.

6. Bring after-game snacks and drinks for the players. Youth teams love to eat a snack after the game. This also creates a time when parents and players can come together and get to know one another. It allows you to compliment the play of others. Focus your comments on team effort, hustle, and improvement the players have made. Congratulate all the players from both teams as you encounter them.

7. Don't analyze or dissect the game or practice for your child in the car ride home. Try very hard not to put pressure on your child to perform, which steals away the fun of the game. Talk in terms of effort and being a team player. Try not to be a continual spectator at your child's practices. This is his or her time to be a kid and they need to learn independence from you. Use father/child and mother/

child time away from the field to practice some of the weaknesses you noticed in the game.

8. Help financially with no strings attached. It you are financially blessed and want to help your child's team with equipment, uniforms, and travel needs, etc., there is nothing wrong with that. But give with a pure heart and don't expect favors in return. See your selfless gift as a way to help all kids.

9. Avoid making negative comments to the umpires. Everyone notes the character of parents who continually badger umpires. Often youth league umpires are teens who are performing a summer job to the best of their ability. If you think you can do a better job, become an umpire yourself. It won't take long for your perspective to change.

10. Fight the trend to specialize in baseball. Use the developmental years to expose your child to a variety of sports and activities. Teams may even call and ask your child to play on fall teams or travel teams, which is flattering. But think about the future. Playing baseball all year has certain short-term benefits and long-term consequences, not to mention the financial commitment that is often associated with it. The more time and money that is invested in baseball, the harder it becomes for parents to keep the game in perspective.

PART THREE

Prepare to Coach

Whether you are an experienced youth league baseball coach or venturing onto the baseball diamond to conduct a T-ball practice for the first time, there is important information that can make your experience more rewarding and enjoyable. As with any worthwhile endeavor, you must invest the time into learning how to conduct a baseball practice for your players to master the correct skills for their age, develop those skills in appropriate drills, and apply those skills to actual game play. However, the most important thing a coach can do is to make the game fun for the players.

The goal of this section is to give you the confidence to be a successful coach. Don't let the fact that there is more than one way to conduct a practice or teach a skill paralyze your ability to coach. Dare to be different. Think outside the box. Make your experience with the kids special. Make the game fun and be a good role model for your players. Win or lose, focus on the positives, sportsmanship, and always try to relate the game back to life. When things are the most intense, smile and tell a joke. It makes all the difference when the kids know you really care about them, and winning is not life and death for the team.

CHAPTER 8

COACHING YOUTH BASEBALL

Myth #1: You must be a former high school, college, or professional baseball player to coach youth baseball.

Secret: *Anyone who cares about children, has the ability to relate to people, and is willing to learn how to teach the appropriate skills for the players' age group has what it takes to be a good youth baseball coach.*

Myth #2: Your team has practiced two times a week to get ready for the season's games. Now that the games have started, there is no need to practice anymore.

Secret: *It is very important to practice before the games begin. However, it is just as critical to practice after the season is underway to focus on the team and individual weaknesses of players. How else will players and teams make the adjustments necessary to improve?*

Myth #3: Without an available baseball field, you can't have baseball practice.

Secret: *With a little creativity, coaches can hold an effective practice just about anywhere. The key is to assess the space that is going to be used, and, with safety as first priority, plan skills and drills that can be effectively accomplished that day.*

THE COMMUNITY COACH

City to city, town to town, it is getting much harder to find people who are willing to take on the rewarding task of coaching amateur baseball teams. Gone are the days when individuals in the community coached youth teams from year to year, providing kids the experience and rewards of participating in America's great pastime. Often, these coaching "mainstays" did not have their own children on their team. Yet, each spring, they could be found coaching a new group of kids who were excited to learn the skills needed to play baseball correctly.

These coaches were motivated by a desire to help kids "grow" through the game of baseball and to give back to the sport they themselves loved as kids. They knew the game and had a passion to see that kids learned the right way to play. They took pride in being prepared and giving the kids their best each time they were together at practice or games.

Most of these individuals no longer tread the green grass and red clay of baseball diamonds across America. They have either passed on or have grown tired of dealing with overzealous parents who think their child is the next Major League star. As a result of the declining numbers of the long-standing youth coach, a new generation of coaches has to step up to the plate.

ARE YOU QUALIFIED TO COACH YOUTH BASEBALL?

Baseball coaches educate themselves on the game of baseball, prepare to relay that information to the players, and disseminate that information with passion, excitement, and energy. Good coaches care about their players, take pride in their team's practices, and commit themselves to having fun with the kids. This type of coach could conceivably lose every game during the season, and his or her team would still have fun and want to play baseball again next year. The coach's kids play to have fun, and winning is usually a direct byproduct of fun!

You don't need to be a former high school, college, or professional baseball player to be an effective youth baseball coach. It only takes a committed person who cares enough about the players to learn the basic skills of the game and to teach them correctly. No one knows everything about baseball. Coaches at all levels must remain open-minded and seek new information related to our nation's great pastime if they are to be the best they possibly can be.

This book and DVD set will give you the confidence to teach the necessary skill mechanics and implement important "game concepts" to your team. When your players receive well-executed repetitions at fun, organized practice, they will improve, respond better in actual game situations, and reduce their incidence of injury.

The Importance of Perspective

As important as it may seem at the time, winning will eventually become secondary to a player's memory of the overall youth baseball experience. The older the players who are competing, the more the score matters, but this should not be at the expense of learning basic skills, techniques, and life lessons through the game of baseball. Thus, it is important never to lose perspective on how influential a coach is in the developmental process of a young person.

Once they become adults, players will often think back on their childhood baseball memories and reflect on their coaches. They will ask themselves questions such as: "Did the coaches make practices and games fun? Did they teach the fundamentals of the game? Were they organized and prepared? Did they care about the team? Did they encourage us? Did they teach sportsmanship? And, if I become a youth baseball coach for my child's team, would I follow the example of any of my coaches?" Keeping in mind these important thoughts should help you maintain the right perspective throughout your coaching stint.

TEACHING FUNDAMENTAL SKILLS

No matter the age of the player you are coaching, you will be able to use some concepts found in this book immediately and save others for future years or higher levels of baseball. Many youth baseball coaches make the choice to move up the ladder with their team as the players grow older and advance in the game. If a youth baseball coach successfully teaches the minimum skill expectation for the current age group, the team will be able to digest more complicated skills and concepts needed at the higher levels of the game. Keep in mind that new players will join the coaches' teams each year. Thus, each coach has the responsibility to teach the game to the newest players and get them caught up with the rest of the team.

A prepared youth baseball coach understands that the game varies greatly based on the age of the participant he or she is coaching. If coaches attempt to teach their players more than they can reasonably handle (for

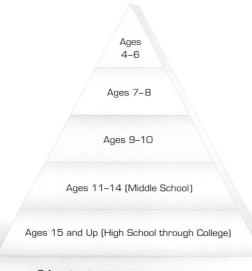

Ages
4–6

Ages 7–8

Ages 9–10

Ages 11–14 (Middle School)

Ages 15 and Up (High School through College)

FIGURE 8.1. The fundamental skills triangle.

their age and cognitive ability), they are preparing them for failure. Baseball skills and game concepts can be very complex, and if players are not ready for the next step, they can suffer higher rates of failure and ruin their fragile confidence level. For example, students learn addition and subtraction before multiplication and division.

The concept of minimum skill expectation by age, or developmentally appropriate skills, can be more easily understood by visualizing a triangle (**Figure 8.1**). At the top or point of the triangle, very little skill must be learned and mastered to be successful playing baseball. This would simulate T-ball or 4- to 6-year-old baseball. However, as the players grow older and advance down the triangle to coach-pitch or machine-pitch baseball, they will be required to learn more advanced skills and game concepts to be successful. The load continues to get larger as they work towards the bottom of the triangle. Once a player reaches the base of the triangle, he or she should be able to learn and implement most of the advanced skills and concepts the game has to offer.

HOW TO CONDUCT A BASEBALL PRACTICE

As mentioned, these days it is common for parents of players to fill the role of coach so a team can exist. Though this is a noble gesture, most of these parents are not prepared to coach, and they are not properly educated by their local recreation departments about how to plan, organize, and conduct a coherent baseball practice. Therefore, each year practices become less organized, increasingly boring, and, very often, counterproductive to improving skill. Participants are not consistently exposed to the fundamentals, drills, and concepts necessary to play the game successfully at their level. A good-quality baseball practice is not defined as one player batting, one getting ready to hit, and the rest of the players standing in the field, bored to death. A constructive practice can be defined as making the best use of available facilities and time to have fun while teaching/practicing appropriate skills, drills, and game concepts to as many players as effectively possible. Players who are not stimulated with an educational, fun practice often end up as unmotivated, under-skilled, bored participants who lose interest in baseball or are not physically or mentally prepared to move up and play at more advanced levels. Let's take a logical look at building a fun, productive, and energetic baseball practice no matter what level of the game you have decided to coach.

A PRACTICE FROM START TO FINISH

The segments that follow are areas that are typically included in a well-planned baseball practice no matter the age or skill level of the team that is being coached. It is not mandatory that coaches spend time in every segment at every practice; however, good coaches generally touch upon these segments most of the time. Because coaches may want to pay more attention to a specific area on a particular day, they may skip or combine certain segments of practice to reach this intended goal. For example, a well-executed team batting practice can cover three segments of practice in one activity. If the team is divided equally into small groups, each group can work on a different skill instead of players standing in the field waiting for a ball to be hit to them.

Some coaches who hold multiple practices a week may choose to have a "focus" for each practice, such as an offensive priority or a defensive priority. Here the coaches spend much more practice time on one segment such as improving offensive skills, defensive skills, or preparing for game situations.

Key #1: State Practice Objectives

(Approximately 3–5 minutes)

When it is time to start practice, gather the players and assistant coaches (parents or helpers) around. Sit the players on the dugout bench or have them take a knee and give you their attention. Quickly review what the team will do for that practice. At this point, you are sharing bulleted information you wrote in your practice plan. Players can then mentally focus on what they need to accomplish for the day. The coach can remind players of situations from recent games that must be addressed, or provide any focus for the team.

Key #2: Execute a Team Stretching Routine
(Approximately 5–10 minutes)

It is vital that every practice begins with a stretching routine. This starts practice in a way that is comfortable for and familiar to all the players, and it serves the functional purpose of preventing possible injury and preparing the body and mind for activity. Exercises should consist of three phases: raising core body temperature, which can be accomplished with a simple lap or two around the field or practice area; dynamic stretching, which is loosening the body through movement patterns; and static stretching, which is holding a specific body position for a period of 15 to 20 seconds. Basic dynamic and static stretching routines can easily be found on the Internet. The important thing is to pick out a few of each that address all the major muscle groups and execute them the correct way, in the same order before every practice and game. When possible, implement some dynamic stretches that will also help players work on coordinating basic movements; these can help them become more athletic.

Key #3: Execute a Team Throwing Routine
(Approximately 10–15 minutes)

The most elementary skills of baseball are throwing and catching. Yet most baseball players do a poor job of both. This includes young and mature participants. Players should possess the ability to consistently throw the ball to an intended target with correct throwing mechanics. They must also be able to consistently catch the baseball with confidence, ease, and control.

A throwing routine has a dual purpose. It warms up the arm to throw, yet it also serves the even more-important function of creating good muscle memory (habits) in the players who execute the drills correctly on a regular basis. Through a progression of these drills, players train their bodies to perform at higher levels. Every defensive player on the field must eventually possess these fundamental skills. Coaches must take the time to teach throwing skills and drills. They must regularly watch players throw to diagnose any throwing and catching flaws that can be eliminated. See the accompanying DVD to learn correct throwing mechanics, basic throwing drills for your target age group, and practice ideas to implement throwing and catching into stations.

Key #4: *Improve Team Baserunning Skills*
(Approximately 10–15 minutes)

Baserunning wins and loses more baseball games at all levels, yet it is typically the most under-coached area of baseball. One reason is that many coaches don't know how to teach it correctly. Another reason is that coaches don't want to take time out of practice to spend on baserunning.

The key is to focus on elementary baserunning vital for your age group or level of play, and figure out a way to get as many repetitions for your players in the shortest amount of time. One suggestion is to use throw-down bases, which can be made (from cardboard squares, for instance) or purchased. Place five bases in line with first base, and make five lines of three players (for a team of 15 players). Now a lot of kids can practice at once. Please see the end of Chapters 1 through 3 for elementary baserunning that must be covered for your age group.

Key #5: *Improve Individual and Team Offense*
(Approximately 15–30 minutes)

The individual and team offense segment of practice can encompass a wide range of offensive drills (such as double tee drill, basketball tee drill, side toss, front toss, etc.) or team batting practice. It is up to each coach to decide which areas to emphasize for the day. The offensive focus for each practice will be based on the age of the players, skill level, or individual and/or team weaknesses that have been exposed by opponents. Specific hitting mechanics, relative practice ideas, and drills can be found in Chapters 1–3 and on the accompanying DVD.

Key #6: *Improve Individual and Team Defense*
(Approximately 15–30 minutes)

The individual and team defense segment of practice encompasses a wide range of defensive skills (for instance, fielding ground balls, catching fly balls, knowing what base to throw to, creating a dead ball, and so on), defensive drills by position (such as short hop drills, 3-step/5-step drill, tree drill, and so on), first base play, and pitchers' bullpens or side work.

It is up to each coach to decide which areas to prioritize for the practice. The defensive focus for each practice will be based on the age of the players, skill level, or individual and/or team weaknesses that have been exposed by opponents. Refer to Chapters 1 through 3 and the enclosed DVD for specific defensive skills, drills, and practice ideas that are appropriate for the age group you are targeting.

Key #7: Cover and Improve Relevant Game Situations
(Approximately 5–10 minutes)

Every level of baseball has relevant game situations that must successfully be handled and executed by the defense in order to effectively compete. Often games in the early part of the season will expose areas that need to be improved. Defensive team plays such as which base to throw the ball to in various situations, or how to create a dead ball to stop play for the offense, are examples of skills that must be taught and then covered in practice to prepare players to help the team win the game. At the lowest level of the game (T-ball), there are very few relevant game situations. Getting an out at first on a routine ground ball will be hard enough. However, as the skill levels of players improve, the number of relevant game situations that a team must be prepared for will significantly increase. The players must also learn specific league rules that apply to their age group.

Key #8: Conclude Practice
(Approximately 5–10 minutes)

When it is time to end the practice, gather the players and assistant coaches (or helpers) around. Instruct the players to sit on the dugout bench or ask them to take a knee and give you their attention. Quickly review the aspects of practice that the team did well. Focus on the positives, but also be honest about team weaknesses that must be improved.

Never use this time to talk about an individual player unless you are giving high praise to a person to give them confidence. Give the team some basic ideas of what they can do on their own to improve their skills before the next practice or game, such as watching specific sections of the enclosed DVD, reviewing their team playbook, or practicing a certain skill. Remind the team of the next practice date and time (or game). Players should then pick up any trash that was created at practice and pack up their gear. Finally, bring the team together and ask everyone to put their hands in the middle of the circle and, on the count of three, yell "Team!" to dismiss the players.

PAY ATTENTION TO PRACTICE DETAILS

As with anything else in life, the more experience you acquire organizing and conducting baseball practices, the better you will become at it. In order to conduct a successful practice, coaches must pay special attention to detail. They must make effective use of practice time, maximize facility space, effectively communicate with others, and make necessary adjustments. Let's take a closer look at each component and see how they can easily and successfully be applied to practice today.

DETAIL #1: PREPARATION

Before practice begins, coaches should sit down and think about what they want to work on with their players and contemplate the most effective ways to accomplish those objectives. Create a written plan. On a piece of paper or an index card, outline the practice from beginning to end in bulleted or outline form. If you have an hour and a half to practice, how much time should you allot for each aspect? For instance, you might allow 5 minutes for warm-up (stretching), 10 minutes for the throwing routine, 30 minutes for three different offensive stations, 30 minutes for three defensive stations, and 15 minutes for game situations.

Ideally it would be a great help if the head coach could send out an e-mail or text to let the assistant coaches or parent helpers know what is in store for practice so they, too, can prepare. The key is to effectively use help to disseminate information, and to engage the players in a fun practice that has purpose! Let's consider some important aspects for your team.

Assess Team and Individual Ability Levels

Coaches should take time at the start of the season to assess the overall skill level of the team to determine which areas of weakness need to be addressed first. The majority of practice time should be focused on teaching and offering drills to improve the fundamental skills of the game such as throwing, catching, fielding, hitting, and baserunning. Once the majority of the players can perform fundamental skills for their age level, more focus can be placed on game basics such as team offense, team defense, and execution of basic game situations.

Learn to Teach the Skills and Drills

Coaches must take some time to learn how the basic fundamental skills and drills of baseball should be correctly taught and performed before they start to teach these skills to their players.

Refer to the appropriate section of the DVD for your age group and select the specific chapter items that cover the skills and drills you want to teach. Misinforming players can lead to years of re-teaching skills and increased failure rates.

Learn to Teach Game Basics

Often coaches do a poor job of teaching players how to perform basic team offenses, defenses, or simple plays that must be executed.

For T-ball or coach-pitch/machine-pitch teams, these game basics are simply where to throw the ball to make simple defensive plays such as force outs, tag outs, or to stop the play (so base runners can no longer advance).

Generally, coaches should wait until the ages of nine and ten to introduce kids to basic offensive plays such as sacrifice bunting and stealing, and basic team defensive plays such as bunt defenses, and simple first and third defensive situations. This is especially true for all-star teams and travel teams. A coach may also want to implement a few basic trick plays that can be used when competing against a poorly coached team.

Coaches should think about the basic offensive, defensive, and possible trick plays that they want their team to learn, and make a basic team playbook. Make copies of the plays with their corresponding names or numbers, and give them to the players to review at home.

Keep in mind that baserunning is the most under-taught aspect of the game at all levels yet it often has the greatest impact on winning and losing close ball games. Don't neglect to use some practice time to cover basic baserunning skills so they will become instinctive for players.

Learn to Teach the League Rules

Each league has specific rules that must be followed for each age group. It is the coach's responsibility to know the basic rules and to teach the relevant ones to their players in practice. Coaches should receive a rulebook or a pamphlet with the league rules that must be followed. They should review those rules and implement situations in practice so the players will become comfortable with the most important rules that directly impact the game.

Learn to Teach the Mental Game

Baseball has both physical and mental components. As players progress through the levels of the game, coaches must continue to help them refine their physical skills. However, once a player reaches the age of nine or ten, he or she should be introduced to the basic mental skills of the game such as how to cope with failure. Players should be taught that it takes a mentally strong person to succeed at baseball.

Make or Find Necessary Equipment

Most leagues provide their coaches with the basic essentials for conducting a practice and game play. These usually include catchers' gear, a few dozen baseballs, a few bats, batters' helmets, and a field to use once or twice a week. Teams that operate outside of a league, such as travel teams, may not have equipment provided for them and may have to purchase or make equipment for an efficient practice.

In order for players to experience the repetition they need to improve, coaches can use some creativity to make equipment. For example, empty gallon paint cans, some PVC pipe, radiator hose, and some ready-mix cement are all that is needed to make a batter's tee. Coaches can also contact local tennis centers to request old used tennis balls. These balls can be used to hit off the tees into a side fence as a drill at practice. Cardboard boxes can be cut into squares and used as throw-down bases for baserunning drills. This allows players to form three or four lines instead of requiring the whole team to line up at one base.

DETAIL #2: USE OF PRACTICE TIME

A coach's ability to effectively use a small amount of time is one of the greatest problems with baseball practices at all levels. In other words, there is far too much wasted time. Coaches must be efficient. Routines must be established for the players. Coaches should make effective use of their help, prioritize what the team needs the most at that point in time, and continue to practice once the season begins.

Establish Routines

The largest amount of wasted time is at the start of the season. Once the team is picked, coaches must take the first few practices to teach and establish routines. This will take more initial time in the beginning of the season but will save a great deal of time in the long run. It will help players improve and create team leadership and discipline.

Initial preparation includes warm-up routines (stretches), throwing routines, drill sequences, batting practice routines, and more. Once players learn specific routines, they will be able to complete more repetitions in the same amount of time

Use Your Help Effectively

Coaches should not try to handle everything on their own. Practices will be slow, boring, and counterproductive if only one person tries to do it all. The idea is for as many players to perform as many skills as possible in the shortest period of time.

If there are not enough assistant coaches to run at least three drill stations at a time, the head coach should solicit help from local high school players or college students who are seeking degrees in physical education, coaching, or parks and recreation. A last resort would be to solicit help from a few parents of players on the team. However, choose this help wisely. Take the initial time to teach volunteers how to run one offensive drill and one defensive drill at practice. Let them watch the DVD, which shows them how to teach the drill and how the drill should look when it is performed correctly. Allow them to coach the same drills at each practice so they will get better at them as the players improve. Once they master the basic level of the drill, they can add more elements to it. Each assistant can eventually learn and implement a total of two or three offensive and defensive drills throughout the season, and practices will become much more productive.

The "spoke and wheel" method is another effective way to teach skills to a team. The head coach teaches elements of the skill to the entire group, including the other volunteers and players. Then, at the appropriate breaking point, the coach splits the players into small groups, which go with one volunteer coach and practice what the whole group learned. After practicing for a set amount of time, all the players and assistant coaches meet with the head coach, who adds more to the skill or moves on to the next fundamental.

Prioritize Practice Objectives

If there is only a limited time to practice, it becomes vital to prioritize the areas of the game that the team needs to work on the most. Teams with players ages four, five, and six (typically T-ball) and ages seven and eight (typically coach- or machine-pitch) should focus a large portion of their practice time on individual fundamental skills such as throwing correctly, catching, fielding, hitting, and running the bases. These are the ages at which players are developing their initial muscle memory (habits). If they can successfully learn to execute basic fundamental skills with good mechanics (proper movement sequencing) then they will have much more fun playing baseball. As coaches progress to the levels of baseball played by nine and ten year olds, the portion of practice that focused on the individual fundamental skills should be reduced, and more time should be allotted to game skills such as team offense, defense, and correctly reacting to various game situations.

Continue to Practice Once the Games Begin

Most coaches see the importance and necessity of practicing with their team before the official season begins. In fact, many leagues provide each team with a minimum of two pre-season practices a week to accomplish this goal. However, once the actual games begin, most leagues and coaches feel that practice time is no longer necessary and they only show up to play opponents. There may also be a shortage of ball fields or facilities at which to hold practice when the playing season is in process, due to the number of games that are played each night. This can deter leagues and coaches from continuing to practice throughout the whole season.

Unfortunately, the limited number of team practices held prior to the games is not nearly enough to correctly teach and reinforce baseball skills. Game play will expose team and individual strengths and weaknesses, but coaches and players should not attempt to fix these weaknesses during the actual games. This is a sure recipe for disaster and it can significantly slow the progress of a player and the team. Players should get to have fun during the actual games. A coach can make minor adjustments based on situations that arise in the game, however, keep in mind that conscious thinking reduces performance levels in baseball. Therefore, players and teams must have practice time that gives them the opportunity to focus on making adjustments. A well-conducted practice will also provide the players or team with the repetitions needed to build the skill to a point where they can have success in future games.

DETAIL #3: USE OF FACILITIES

Many coaches become paralyzed when they feel they don't have adequate facilities for team practice. Because of misconceptions of what a baseball practice should look like, they don't have the creativity and vision to organize an efficient baseball practice anywhere they can find a vacant space. With safety as the primary concern, good coaches can use modified space and equipment, and get more done in one hour than a coach who has access to the nicest baseball field in the community.

Safety

Baseball contains inherent risks of injury to its participants, coaches, and even parents who watch practices and games. However, coaches should never put their players in a situation where they are at increased risk of injury. Thus, when coming up with creative ideas for your team to practice, in the absence of an actual baseball field, a coach must think of all the ways that players might be at risk. If that risk can't be reasonably eliminated, that idea, facility, or open space should be discarded as a possible choice for practice.

Coaches should take out supplemental insurance to cover the risk of liability to their team, especially if these coaches are offering unique solutions to the trend of minimized practice sessions. This offers protection, not only from potential injury, but also from legal actions contemplated by misunderstanding or misguided parents.

Be Creative

Coaches must avoid thinking that they need an actual baseball field to hold an effective practice. A coach can find indoor cages, an outdoor cage at a player or friend's house, an available gym, empty flat lots, football fields, soccer fields, an open space at a nearby park, or anywhere else that does not pose an added risk for injury to the players, coaches, or parents in attendance.

Coaches should assess any potential facility or space and decide what can safely and reasonably be accomplished there. Work into the drills restricted-flight baseballs, tennis balls, tape balls, Wiffle balls, Wiffle golf balls, or similar. Teach hitting, bunting, fielding, pitching, team defense, team offense, baserunning, trick plays, throwing mechanics, throwing drills, and so on. You do not need a field to teach the team the stretching and throwing routines that will be used in each and every practice and game. The options are endless!

In order to keep players, coaches, and parents safe at your practices, make sure they are using the proper equipment for the space. Err on the side of caution.

DETAIL #4: EFFECTIVE COMMUNICATION

Coaches must be able to communicate and work with people. It is the nature of the job. Coaches will routinely interact with league officials, assistant coaches, parents, umpires, other coaches, facility coordinators, and their players. It takes effective verbal and non-verbal communication to disseminate information to all these sources.

Expectations

In order to maintain successful practices, parents must be kept up to speed about the time and location of workouts, and advised what they should do in the event of adverse weather, make-up practices, or any other change in plans. Parents should also be made aware of the expectations of the coach since the parents are responsible for their children getting to practices and games on time and, in many cases, raising money for the team. Thanks to mass communication methods, it is easier than ever for coaches to keep everyone on the same page

Head coaches must communicate well with assistant coaches, volunteer parent helpers, the players' parents, and the players themselves about what the team will focus on for each practice. People will respond favorably to a coach who regularly and clearly sets forth his or her expectations for the team.

Be Positive

Baseball is a sport of failure. The game is full of failed attempts at hitting, throwing strikes, scoring runs, and so on. Players of all ages need a coach who communicates in a positive way. This includes verbal and non-verbal communication. What we do often speaks louder than what we say. Players will enjoy participating in practice when it is organized, high intensity, on task, and fun. I can't remember the last time I had fun being around a negative person. Baseball coaches should always remain positive, especially when disappointments occur.

Show the Skill

Most people are visual learners. Therefore, do not spend an inordinate amount of time talking about skills or drills. This is boring for players, especially very young participants. The kids signed up to play baseball, not to be lectured about the sport. Yes, there are times when coaches have to talk in order to teach, just try not to spend more than 5 to10 minutes at a time talking. Players want to hit, field, and throw. If one of your players executes a skill correctly, let him or her demonstrate to the rest of the team.

Consistent Teaching and Terminology

Inconsistent instruction and use of terminology confuses players and significantly slows their progress. Unfortunately, this is a common problem. Players who are trying to conceptualize a complex game of intricate skills are often confused by the lingo that coaches use to describe nuances of the skills. Also, differing philosophies can cause certain coaches to completely change the mechanics of a player. This re-learning can cause players to take steps backward, especially when the new technique is not necessarily fundamentally sound. In order to make the best use of time, it is helpful if the coaches of each league agree upon a consistent method of teaching the fundamental skills of the game. It is vital that all coaches within a team use consistent teaching techniques and terminology.

Teach Your Helpers Their Responsibilities

If you are fortunate enough for volunteers or hired assistants to help you with practice, it is vital to let them know well in advance exactly what they are responsible for teaching or what drills they are responsible for running. Refer them to the DVD for the appropriate age group to learn the skills. You can send them a practice schedule via e-mail or text message to give them time to plan out how they want to implement expectations.

DETAIL #5: MAKE ADJUSTMENTS

Baseball, like life, is a game of adjustments. No matter how much planning you do, things will rarely go exactly as you anticipate. Coaches must be able to think on their feet. Be creative. When dealing with people, one thing is for sure: nothing is certain. Try to consider the following factors when planning a practice: poor weather, small numbers at practice, not enough time, lack of help, late or absent coaches, late players, lack of equipment, lack of adequate facilities, players on the team below the skill level for their age, and so on.

SKELETON PRACTICES

Below you will find three skeleton practices for each age group covered in this book. They are meant to give you an effective framework. Nothing is set in stone except that every practice should begin with stated objectives from the coach and include a stretching and throwing routine, as discussed earlier in the chapter.

T-Ball Practice: 1 hour

3 minutes: State practice objectives in very simple terms.
7 minutes: Stretching as a team.

- A. Coach leads warm-up lap.
- B. Coach leads simple dynamic movements (skipping, slides, etc.).
- C. Coach leads simple static stretches for the arms.

15 minutes: Throwing and catching skills (three stations of 5 minutes each).

- A. Coach throws tennis balls to players' glove-side only.
- B. Players take turns throwing to a coach.
- C. Coach visually checks each player's grip of the ball and makes adjustments. Then the coach teaches the simple cues of "step," "power," and "throw," working on throwing tennis balls into a fence.

15 minutes: Offensive rotation (three stations of 5 minutes each).

- A. Coach works on teaching players how to set up correctly to the tee.
- B. Coach uses five tees and tennis balls, and players hit into the fence on command to swing.
- C. Coach teaches players how to hit off the batting tee and run through first base.

15 minutes: Defensive rotation (three stations of 5 minutes each).

- A. Coach teaches players how to field the ball by letting the ball (mouse) roll into the glove (mousetrap). Then the coach rolls soft baseballs gently to players, who attempt to field and throw back to the coach.
- B. Coach gently tosses tennis balls to the players' glove-sides, simulating a gentle fly ball.

C. Coach rolls soft baseballs to players' sides so they have to move a few feet to the ball, and throw it back to the coach or the two or three players on the team who will likely play first base.

5 minutes: Baserunning.

A. Baserunning tag: Coaches set up players on each base and between the bases. When they say "go," players start to run around the bases counter-clockwise (first base, second base, third base, home plate). They must touch each base as they try to race to touch the person in front of them. If they successfully touch the player in front of them, that person is out and they keep going until there is a winner or a select number of players left untagged. Players should be continually moved so the fastest players on the team cannot repeatedly tag the same players out at the start of the race.
B. Timed home runs: Time players running from home to home to see who can run the fastest.

Conclude practice.

Coach-Pitch or Machine-Pitch Practice: 1 hour, 30 minutes

3 minutes: State practice objectives in very simple terms.
5 minutes: Stretching as a team.

A. Team warm-up lap.
B. Coach leads simple dynamic movements (skipping, slides, and so on).
C. Coach leads simple static stretches for the arms.

15 minutes: Throwing and catching skills (three stations of 5 minutes each).

A. Coach throws soft baseballs to glove-side and to backhand.
B. Players execute simple throwing drills with each other:
Sitting wrist flip.
Standing power position.
C. Coach throws tennis balls to players who run short distances to their glove-side to make the catch.

30 minutes: Offensive rotation (three stations of 10 minutes each).

A. Coach uses batting tees for players to hit from with focus on establishing a routine entering the batter's box that includes placing the back foot in the batter's box first, checking for a proper grip, plate coverage, and a fundamental swing. Players execute a swing on the coach's command and repeat the process.
B. Coach lets players hit live off machine or coach on the field.
C. Coach feeds players front toss or side toss with restricted-flight balls.

30 minutes: Defensive rotation (three stations of 10 minutes each).

A. Infield ground balls: Coach teaches players how to charge the ball and field the ball by creating a simple fielding triangle. Then the coach hits soft baseballs gently to players, who attempt to field and throw back to the coach or a player at first base.
B. Outfield fly balls: Coach throws low-level pop-ups with tennis balls, focusing on keeping the player relatively stationary. Coach emphasizes that players catch the ball with both hands in front of their body.
C. Fielding and throwing to bases: Coach sets up two lines of players, one at shortstop and the other at second base. Players are placed at first and second base to receive throws. The coach hits ground balls, alternately to each line, the players move to field the ball. The line at second throws to first base and the line at shortstop throws to second base. After 5 minutes, the fielders playing second can throw to second base and the fielders playing shortstop can throw to first base.

7 minutes: Baserunning

A. Coach instructs players to run from home plate to first base. The coach at first base lets the players run through first base or verbally communicates, with accompanying body language, that the player must keep running to second base.
B. Coach instructs players to run from first to second base, and players must look at the third base coach to determine whether they should stop at second base or continue on to third base.

Conclude practice.

Player-Pitch Practice: 1 hour, 30 minutes

3 minutes: State practice objectives.

10 minutes: Stretching as a team.

   A. Warm-up lap.
   B. Dynamic stretching routine to prepare the body for movement.
   C. Static stretches to loosen the arms.

10 minutes: Throwing routine.

   A. Sitting wrist flip: 1 minute.
   B. Kneeling figure eight: 1 minute.
   C. Kneeling power position: 1 minute.
   D. Standing figure eight: 1 minute.
   E. Standing power position: 1 minute.
   F. Boxers: 1 minute.
   G. Jumpbacks: 1 minute.
   H. Throwing long: 3 minutes.

30 minutes: Offensive rotation (three stations of 10 minutes each).

   A. Double tee drill.
   B. Leads: Teach players how to take leads and how to read a basic pick-off move from a pitcher if the league allows leads and/or base stealing.
   C. Front toss on field.

30 minutes: Defensive rotation (three stations of 10 minutes each).

   A. Infielding: Fielding mechanics drill.
   B. Outfield: Fly ball pattern drill.
   C. Pitchers: T drill (not to be confused with "hitting tee" drills).

7 minutes: Game Situations.

   A. Review signs that will be given from the third base coach. Make sure players know their meaning.
   B. Ask a few players to take turns giving signs to the team to demonstrate understanding.

Conclude practice.

PART FOUR

Travel and All-Star Teams

Travel and all-star teams offer new challenges that are different than the standard recreational baseball leagues. Most recreational teams are made up of players of all ability levels who typically are registered by their parents to play a short season of 10 to 15 games. The children are guaranteed playing time based on rules established by their league officials and enforced by umpires and coaches. Recreational teams typically practice one to two times a week before the games begin, and many teams will not practice again after that.

Travel baseball teams are typically assembled from a tryout in which the best players are selected from a geographical area. All-star teams often are made up of the best players from their league, and are usually chosen by their coach based on performance in the recreational league's regular season games.

Both of these types of teams tend to practice as many as four times a week before the actual games are played, and travel teams may even practice several months in the off-season in preparation for competitive game play. Both travel ball and all-star teams are serious about winning and in most cases will play substantially more games than the average recreational team. Some travel teams, bent on playing as much baseball as possible, will compete in weekend tournaments, playing in more than 60 games through the spring and summer and another 25 to 30 in the fall. All-star teams tend to play in series of tournaments, which they must continue to win (starting with localized tournaments) in order to qualify for state play, regional play, and eventually national play. A poor showing at any tournament spells the end of the road for an all-star team and their season is over.

In many cases, travel baseball teams have substantial budgets and require the parents to pay out-of-pocket or raise the money for their child to participate. It is not unusual for each family to contribute thousands of dollars, not including the expenses of traveling to tournaments and staying in hotels. These teams, most often, are coached by individuals, usually paid, with some type of coaching credentials. Their duties include handling the administrative tasks associated with planning, organizing, and coordinating fundraisers; scheduling tournaments, departure, and arrival times; making hotel reservations; and tending to game-by-game details.

In comparison, all-star teams are usually financially supported by their league. However, it is not uncommon for teams to raise additional funds to help offset the costs of participating in tournaments, including travel and accommodation expenses. All-star teams are coached by volunteers, who are chosen by how well their teams placed in the regular season. For example, the head coach of the all-star team probably finished first in the league, and their assistant coaches likely finished second, third, and so on. Because of all these factors, travel baseball and all-star teams have their own unique set of obstacles and concerns that must be successfully addressed if the players are going to develop the physical and mental skills needed to advance in this sport.

CHAPTER 9

HOW TO START A TRAVEL BASEBALL TEAM

Myth #1: TRAVEL BASEBALL IS A BETTER CHOICE FOR CHILDREN THAN YOUR LOCAL PARKS AND RECREATION BASEBALL.

Secret: *There are many recreational baseball teams across America and, in many cases, recreational baseball is the best option for players and their families. Travel baseball is not ideal for very young players, players of average ability level, or players who do not have a desire to practice and play games on a regular basis.*

Myth #2: IF THE RECREATIONAL TEAM REGULARLY KEEPS MY CHILD SITTING ON THE BENCH, I'D BE BETTER OFF STARTING A TRAVEL TEAM SO HE OR SHE CAN PLAY ALL THE TIME.

Secret: *It is not proper motivation to start a travel team simply because your child is not getting the playing time or the position you feel he or she deserves. A great deal of effort goes into starting a travel baseball team. Disgruntled parents who attempt to start their own teams usually end up frustrating numerous families and players, and the teams may disintegrate very quickly.*

Myth #3: WHEN PUTTING TOGETHER A TRAVEL TEAM, FAMILIES THAT CANNOT AFFORD THE EXPENSES SHOULD BE AVOIDED.

Secret: *Very competitive travel teams desire to have the best talent in their area regardless of financial status. There are ways to make positions on a travel team available to the financially disadvantaged. It just takes some creativity. A player should never be denied a baseball experience due to lack of money!*

CONSIDERATIONS FOR STARTING A TRAVEL TEAM

Travel baseball is not the best option for every player. For example, most kids under the age of ten are generally too young to benefit from a travel team. A short all-star schedule at the conclusion of their recreational season is even pushing it for T-ball and coach-pitch/machine-pitch players. However, if the goal is to create a travel baseball experience for preteen players and their families, there is a great deal of planning that should precede sending out invitations or conducting tryouts.

Travel teams that pop up because parents are disgruntled with their child's playing time generally cause more problems than they are worth. However, a well-planned team can stand the test of time and provide years of top-notch baseball instruction and competition for the players involved. The fact is that running a first-class travel baseball team, at any level, is a lot of hard work.

ORGANIZATIONAL MEETINGS

The first step is to set up an organizational meeting with other people who may also be interested in starting a travel team. Set some basic objectives and goals for the team. Be sure that everyone is on the same page and has the same expectations. Someone must be in charge of or take over the initial leadership of the team, and it is vital that the purpose for the team's creation is legitimate and well defined. Items that must be discussed and agreed upon include: how the team is going to be selected; how many games or tournaments the team will play; what times of year the team will play; who will coach the team; how many assistant coaches will be hired; how the team will be funded; who will handle the administrative duties, and so on. With an increasing demand being placed on parks and recreation and school facilities, where is your team going to practice or play games? Do you have to reserve those facilities in advance? Is there a fee? Will you have to show proof of insurance? These are all crucial issues that must be agreed upon up front, otherwise the team is sure to dissolve or implode over time from a lack of focus on its direction.

HIRING A QUALIFIED HEAD COACH
AND ASSISTANTS

To start a travel team, you must have coaches. To start a *good* travel team, you must have qualified coaches. To start a *great* travel team, you should have highly qualified coaches who are paid and not related to any of the players! Ultimately, the team will be only as good as the staff. Teams with talented players and a weak staff may win many games because of raw ability. But they will not improve to the level they otherwise would have if they were under knowledgeable coaches who could help them "polish up" the little things that often make the difference at the higher levels of the game.

Do you want a head coach who you can control and manipulate, or one who will act in the best interest of the team? Do you want a coach who can teach the game and run an organized practice or one who can only make game decisions? Regardless of these criteria, you should hire a positive coach who loves kids and the game of baseball. To get the best coach available, you will probably have to pay a salary. Coaches have bills too. As with anything else in life, you get what you pay for. Research the coach well and be sure he or she can meet the expectations of the team.

Travel baseball is different than recreational baseball in many ways; you will need a coach who can organize many elements of a team and also manage the parents. Parents will be involved in fundraising, at the very least, and probably in many other aspects of the team as well. Coaches who are paid fairly and not tied to the team through their children may be available for years to come. A parent who coaches the team will probably follow his or her child up the ladder of baseball, and this team will need to look for a new coach next year and perhaps even dissolve.

Once the head coach has been chosen and hired, he or she should have input into who their assistant coaches will be. Positive chemistry among coaches is vital to having a top-notch team. Try to avoid using parents of players on the team as assistants because of the political implications. In short, the other parents will eventually become jealous of these parents being "on the inside." Unless you are going to pay the assistant coaches very well, the situation might require some compromise. Qualified coaches with free time, knowledge, and motivation are not always available in every community. Thus, if you must, get parents of players to help assist with the team, but remember that you will eventually be putting out fires on a regular basis.

TEAM BUDGETS

Every team should have a designated person, other than a coach, who is responsible for the team checkbook and bank account. This creates an accountability system within the team that can prevent the coach from being accused of taking money or using team money inappropriately. If possible, the money should be entrusted to a parent who has integrity and experience with banking. There should be at least two other people on the account at the bank who can sign for checks, and two signatures should be required for each check or withdrawal to reduce the risk of tampering.

Once the team is established, the team accountant should provide weekly updates through financial reports to keep everyone informed about the progress of the budget. These can be sent via e-mail. The coaches should create and present the estimated budgets for the team. These should officially be presented to all the parents who will be helping with the fundraising, and if necessary, modified and voted on.

The individual cost per player should be determined for those parents who prefer to write a check instead of spending the time to raise funds for their children to be on the team. It should also be determined who will be responsible for raising the money to meet the budget. Line items should include, but are not limited to, coaches' salaries, insurance, field rental, uniforms, equipment, fees for setting up bank and checking accounts, tournament entry fees, organization registration fees, umpires for home games, travel expenses (vans, gas, and such), hotels, team meals, fees for filing for tax-exempt status, creating sponsor banners, first-aid kits, score books, etc.

Each of the line items above can be broken down into more detail. Uniforms, for example, can include (home and away) game T-shirts or jerseys, hats, game pants, belts, socks, sleeves, team bags, batting helmets, and so on. Some travel teams can operate on a budget of a couple thousand dollars or less, whereas other teams may require $15,000 to $50,000 to operate successfully. It depends upon each team's goals and expectations. Rising gas prices, for instance, directly impact team and family budgets for travel. Also, specific dollar amounts should be established for minimum petty purchases, and any expenses over the set amount should require an official team vote. All aspects of the team's finances should be determined at its inception and strictly adhered to.

If the team has a very small budget, at the least, it should consider purchasing good-looking uniforms. Teams that feel good about themselves play better and are given initial respect. This does not mean going out and purchasing top-of-the-line name-brand uniforms that will dissolve the team budget. It simply means wearing matching pants, socks, belts, hats, and jerseys. These outfits can consist of a nice T-shirt, a simple adjustable belt, socks to match the belt, plain white baseball pants, and a nice-looking adjustable hat. Or, if the budget allows, purchase full game uniforms from a local sporting goods store or uniform manufacturer. Teams that play travel baseball generally look top-notch. The players' appearance makes a statement that they are serious about winning, and this look is a reflection of the organization. It will be hard to entice talented players to try out for the team if the players don't look sharp, play well, and, in many cases, have a reputation for winning with a first-class coaching staff.

Tax-Exempt Status

Serious travel teams that carry large budgets should consider filing for tax-exempt status as a not-for-profit organization. If the goal of the team is to continue year after year, paying the initial filing fee will probably be necessary to entice investors or large donors to give substantial sums of money in sponsorships. Once the organization qualifies as tax exempt, investors can write off their investment to the team. Filing for tax-exempt status with the Internal Revenue Service will require doing paperwork and paying a hefty fee. It will become vital that records are kept accurately for possible IRS audits. Check with your local IRS office for specifics on tax exemption requirements.

Insurance

It is important to carry an insurance policy to protect players and families involved with the team in the event of an emergency or unforeseen tragedy. You can contact your local insurance agency or search online for "baseball team insurance." Find a company that is reasonable and trustworthy to pay in the event of an emergency. Make sure you are accurate, honest, and thorough when completing necessary forms. Select a policy that will cover all your team's specific needs.

TRYOUTS OR INVITATIONS

One of the first obstacles that must be overcome when starting a travel team is to determine how and when the team will be selected.

- Will the team be chosen based upon accepted invitations to play, or will an open tryout be conducted?
- If the former, how do you determine who gets an invitation?
- What if the invitations are turned down?
- If you are holding an open tryout, how will the tryout be conducted?
- Do you have permission to use a facility for a tryout?
- Do you have insurance in the event of an injury?
- Do you have alternate plans for bad weather?
- Is one day enough time to evaluate the talent?
- What if a very good player can't make the tryout?
- What will serve as proof of a child's age?
- How many players are going to make the alternate list in the event a selected player cannot play?

Many more questions will arise, and those in charge must be ready to answer those questions.

If tryouts are conducted, coaches should evaluate the players on a written scale using justifiable, measurable information to back up their decisions for accepting or rejecting a player. It should be stated up front how and when the players or their parents will be notified of team selections. The coach may consider making phone calls or sending letters to the players who do not make the team. He or she must determine how much time players will be given to make a commitment to the team, once notified of acceptance, before they lose their spot on the roster. How much nonrefundable money will be needed to reserve a roster spot? Other vital questions must be answered before the selection process begins.

Once the team is selected and commitments are made, a parent meeting should be held to cover specific agenda items; team administrators and coaches can field questions. Some parents may later decline their child's participation once they understand the level of commitment (financial and otherwise) required for the team.

COMMITMENT FEES AND FUNDRAISERS

Commitment is not a popular word in today's culture. New travel teams are starting all the time, and the grass might appear greener somewhere else. Disheartened parents are likely to change their minds, especially when they are frustrated with their child's playing time or the coach. The key to any successful travel team is to receive a financial commitment from the families that make up the team.

Commitment fees should be expected for one full season, and the amount should be determined at the first parental meeting. The commitment fee can be collected at once or broken up into payments that must be paid in full by the first two to three months of the season. The commitment fee should be a reasonable amount, but not so much as to put families under financial stress. It should be enough money to keep families from jumping ship mid-voyage, and, as a result, putting the team in a bind. A contract could be signed stipulating that all fees are to be forfeited to the organization if a child quits the team for any reason before the end of the stated season.

In addition to commitment fees, parents are usually expected to participate in team fundraising efforts and/or to solicit sponsors to offset budget costs. (See Chapter 11 for more information on fundraising for travel teams.) One way to encourage a parent to participate in fundraising is to divide the team budget by the number of players. That fractioned amount is technically what each family is responsible for raising. If a family that is financially blessed decides to write a check for their portion then that can be considered by those in charge.

It is usually helpful for all the players to participate in team fundraisers, such as car washes, bake sales, product sales, hosting tournaments, horse shows, golf tournaments, and so on. This creates pride, camaraderie, and ownership in the team. Encourage the parents to let their child participate in these events whenever reasonable. It can improve players' social skills to communicate what they are selling and why they are raising money.

Sponsorships are a great way to get larger investments for your team with fewer "door to door" sales. There are a variety of ways to solicit sponsorships. One way is to offer team banners that are divided into sponsorship levels such as platinum, gold, silver, and bronze. The banners are taken with the team to all games and hung in a visible area at the field, usually behind the team dugout, for all to see.

Scholarships are monies made available to cover the cost of players whose families cannot afford to be involved with travel baseball due to financial strains or other reasons. People in the community may be willing to offset the costs associated so that players will be given the opportunity to participate. Generous individuals who are financially blessed with successful business are sometimes willing to front some or all of the cost of a player who can't afford to participate.

WHERE ARE YOU GOING TO PLAY?

It is important that the tournament and game schedule is planned out well in advance of the actual season. There are many organizations that sponsor youth tournaments such as Amateur Athletic Union (AAU) or United States Specialty Sports Association (USSSA), as well as others. These organizations typically require teams to officially register with them, and they call for specific paperwork, such as birth certificates, proof of team insurance, entry fees, and so on, to be eligible to play in their tournaments. Most youth baseball organizations that host baseball tournaments have varying levels or tiers of difficulty. This means that within travel baseball, some teams are superior in talent to others, and these typically play in the best tournaments. In addition, there is usually a qualification standard that must be met by winning preliminary tournaments before a team is eligible to play in sponsored regional or national tournaments. Some select tournaments will invite the top teams in an age group to take part based on a team's reputation for winning or for fielding a very competitive team.

Team organizers and/or coaches should map out a challenging schedule of tournaments that will allow for team goals to be reached. Challenge your team to get better by playing very good competition, but be realistic as to what tournaments you enter. Avoid the temptation of entering your team in a tournament in which the players have the potential to be humiliated. This will cause the team to take unnecessary steps backward in its development and growth. Players must learn to handle winning and losing, but they should never learn to accept losing as an expected outcome. There is a specific team mentality associated with being the underdog and a separate mentality associated with the expectation to win. Try to put your team in tournaments where it will learn to conquer both mentalities, depending on the weekend's competition.

POSSIBLE CONFLICTS WITH TRAVEL TEAMS

Sometimes coaches and team administrators can become shortsighted when starting or implementing a travel baseball team. There are other teams at all levels playing baseball around the country. When starting a travel team, you must take these other teams into consideration. Failure to do so can create serious conflicts with leagues, coaches, parents, and even your own players. Your players will probably play for their school teams or other recreational teams (baseball, football, basketball, soccer, and so on) sometime during the calendar year. Thus, when scheduling tournaments, games, and practices for your travel team, consider other athletic teams and their coaches. You may have a few families whose kids play on two or three different teams, and they try to successfully juggle them all. These situations will eventually come to a head. There is no way a player can be fully committed to two or three teams. Someone is going to get the short end of the stick. The player is likely to get pressure from all his or her coaches to be committed to their particular team, and it can put the player in an uncomfortable position.

School baseball is played in the spring, and it should be the first priority for the ballplayers when they are in season. This will usually only affect kids in the middle school or high school age group. School baseball teams will naturally have practices and games. The pitchers on your team will probably be the same pitchers as on the school teams. One way to create a major conflict and lose support for your team is to over-pitch a player who is being counted on to pitch for his school ball team. Pitching conflicts make coaches very angry and can ultimately cause serious injury to the innocent player torn between two teams.

Some of your athletes will play other sports for their schools or for their parks and recreation departments in the fall and winter. You will upset the coach of another team if players are being pulled away from him or her for a sport that is out of season. The challenge of any travel team is to find players and families who will only commit to one team at a time. This might not be a realistic expectation for today's players and their families, but the line has to be drawn somewhere. What team can operate successfully if it doesn't know who is going to show up on game day?

CHAPTER 10

MANAGE A WINNING STAFF

Myth #1: A GOOD TRAVEL TEAM OR ALL-STAR TEAM COACH DOES NOT NEED ASSISTANT COACHES TO BE 100 PERCENT EFFECTIVE.

Secret: *Coaches of teams at all levels should ideally use qualified assistants to be fully effective. This is especially true at practice, where it becomes nearly impossible to get the most out of a baseball team without assistance.*

Myth #2: IT'S OKAY FOR COACHES TO TAKE ATTENTION AWAY FROM THEIR OWN FAMILIES TO HELP OTHERS IMPROVE AND PLAY THE GAME OF BASEBALL.

Secret: *This statement could not be more false. However, there are plenty of overzealous coaches who do sacrifice their own families in order to be involved in baseball. This is very sad because the first priority of spouses or parents is to spend meaningful time with their own family.*

Myth #3: TEAMS SHOULD HIRE COACHES BASED SOLELY ON THE LEVEL OF BASEBALL THEY PLAYED.

Secret: *It never hurts to employ coaches with names recognizable in the game of baseball or to hire staff that has played the game at a very high level. However, it is more important to make sure these coaches are reputable people who know how to teach the skills of the game, organize an effective practice, and possess the organizational and administrative talents needed to coordinate a travel team.*

ONLY AS GOOD AS THEIR STAFF

The age or difficulty level of baseball will impact how many assistant coaches your team needs. Most recreational youth teams have a head coach and an assistant coach. Many times the assistant coach will be a parent of a player on the team. All-star teams and travel teams can have upwards of three to five coaches.

No matter how much knowledge, passion, and drive the head coach possesses, the team can only be as good as the entire staff. The head coaches can't do all the coaching on their own or they will eventually lose effectiveness and burn out. The goal of every head coach should to be to locate and hire capable assistant coaches. Jerry Meyers, Head Coach at Old Dominion University in Virginia, states, "It is crucial to surround yourself with good people, communicate the desired direction clearly, and work at it every day."

Qualified assistant coaches are hard to find and even harder to keep because they often have the goal of becoming head coaches or have responsibilities that keep them otherwise occupied. If the head coaches of travel teams can hire and keep assistants on their staff for a number of years then they have a great nucleus to build a consistent winning program. Once a coach establishes a winning travel team program, others will seek to join his or her staff so they can learn from that coach.

A creative head coach can locate people in the area who will be willing to help coach the team. These can include recently graduated high school or college baseball players, students from a nearby college who are in the physical education department, local former pro players, or men and women in the community with baseball experience. Finding such individuals only requires making a few phone calls. If that doesn't work, simply locate individuals willing to learn, or, as a last resort, seek out parents of the players.

It is not necessary to hire the most knowledgeable assistant coaches. If the head coach is dedicated, he or she can successfully teach an assistant coach who is hard-working, loyal, and willing to learn. It is ideal for a top-notch travel team to include coaches responsible for each major component of the game, for instance, a pitching coach, a hitting coach, a fielding coach, and so on. Of course, at the recreational level, coaches do the best job they can with the resources that are available to them. If parents are willing to volunteer, they can be taught to run a simple drill or station at practice.

Loyalty

The fastest way for a baseball team to implode is for an assistant coach or coaches to undermine the head coach. Assistant coaches should "bleed" team colors and stand behind the head coach and his or her decisions, especially in the public eye. Weak-minded assistant coaches will become the target of parents who seek answers for and reasons behind coaching decisions. An assistant coach who lacks loyalty will change the head coach's job description from a baseball coach to firefighter—spending valuable time putting out fires within the program. Assistants at any level of baseball must be loyal to the team at all times. They should never utter a negative word about the program or the staff.

COMPLEMENT STRENGTHS WITH ASSISTANT COACHES

The more competent hands at practice, the more efficient practice becomes. It is vital to the success of the team that the coach's skills are complemented with capable assistant coaches. If a head coach is best at teaching hitting and playing infield, he or she should hire a pitching coach, catching coach (to work with the catcher position), and outfield specialist.

Once a qualified staff is hired, the head coach should not micromanage the assistants; they should be allowed to do their job. When responsibility can be divided among worthy people, more work gets done and the whole team benefits. At the recreational level, practices are more successful when planned out, organized, and sufficient help is available to execute the drills or activities. Implement drills that are easy to teach and produce tangible results. Try to keep the same help on the same drills, week after week, so assistants can get comfortable teaching and managing a station. Encourage team helpers to spend some time reviewing this book and watching the DVD to learn more about what they are trying to teach.

LOSS OF PRIORITIES

Coaches who are committed to their players and determined to build a winning program can easily lose perspective on life outside of baseball. Unmarried coaches can be more focused with their time without hurting others. However, once a coach is married, his or her priorities should change. It takes a very special person to be the spouse of a dedicated baseball coach.

Spouses will spend many lonely nights while their coaching counterparts dedicate themselves to the worthy cause of developing kids. The coach's relentless focus on baseball over time puts a serious strain on a marriage. If the coach has children, then another element of commitment must be met at home. What good is it for baseball coaches to win games and help other kids if they lose their own family in the process? Coaches' teams are not more important than their spouses and children.

Coaches who have given their lives to everyone but their own families tell the saddest stories. One day they wake up to realize that their little boys or girls are all grown up, and the children really don't know their mommy or daddy because they were too busy spending time with everyone else's kids.

CERTIFICATION AND BACKGROUND CHECKS

Many recreation leagues now require volunteer, community, or lay coaches to participate in coaching certification courses. Recreational baseball leagues, all-star teams, and travel baseball teams should require all their coaches to undergo background checks by their local law enforcement office. This may initially insult volunteers who want to assist your team, but they should respect your wishes. Parents want to protect their children and decrease the risk of lawsuits resulting from inappropriate behavior by volunteers.

THE COMMUNICATION FACTOR

Over the course of a season there will be good times, hard times, and sad times. As with any organization, proficient communication is needed for long-term success. A baseball staff resembles a healthy family. You must be able to share openly and "agree to disagree" on differences of opinion. Everyone should direct his or her efforts towards making the experience of the players fun and rewarding.

Coaching styles will play a factor in the efficiency and authenticity of communication. A head coach who uses a dictatorial approach with his or her team and staff will often intimidate the assistant coaches. They will do exactly what the head coach says and will be hesitant to give input about what they think can be improved. The "dictator-style" coach can win games, but his or her assistants might feel as though they are puppets. A coach who actively seeks suggestions from assistant coaches will create staff members who feel they have contributed to the overall success of the team. This type of openness is rewarding, fosters unity, and keeps the communication channels open from top to bottom and bottom to top.

STAFF MEETINGS

It is vital for travel teams to hold regular staff meetings before and during the season. This allows the head coach to communicate his or her expectations to the staff and to assign them individual responsibilities. Areas of concern can also be shared during this time. An experienced coach will recognize or sense when something is bothering one or more staff members. This coach will encourage the staff to clear the air and get the issues out in the open to be resolved. A staff member who harbors hard feelings can be as much of a bad influence as a player with a bad attitude. Assistant coaches, especially inexperienced ones, will openly welcome direction, but should also be given the freedom to implement their own style. Each player on a team provides different strengths and weaknesses. The same is true for coaches. Staff meetings can also be used to set direction for the team's upcoming season, including setting up practice schedules; discussing starting lineups, season theme and goals; assigning players' roles, coaches' responsibilities, and more.

ASSISTANT COACHES HAVE LIVES, TOO

Assistant coaches are at the disposal of the head coach and his or her practice and game schedules. There will be times when practices run late, but head coaches cannot make this a routine. Create a practice schedule that is direct and focused. At the travel team level, two hours is the longest an average practice should run. The players will respond to fun, high-energy practices, and your assistant coaches will thank you for keeping their spouses and children happy.

CHAPTER 11

FUNDRAISING

Myth #1: REGISTRATION FEES PROVIDE ALL THE MONEY AN ALL-STAR OR TRAVEL TEAM NEEDS TO OFFER AND OPERATE A FIRST-CLASS EXPERIENCE FOR THE KIDS.

Secret: *It takes a lot of money to run a top-notch all-star or travel baseball team. Often this money must be raised in addition to initial registration fees through extensive fundraising efforts.*

Myth #2: BOOSTER CLUBS RISK BEING OVERTAKEN BY PARENTS WHO SEEK CONTROL AND POWER.

Secret: *Booster clubs, if run correctly, are a chance for all the players' parents to work together to improve the experience for the team. It takes the help of everyone, while keeping the purpose of the club in the forefront of the parents' minds, for the booster club to be fully functional.*

Myth #3: FUNDRAISING SHOULD ONLY BE DONE BY PARENTS. THE KIDS WILL BENEFIT FROM THE PARENTS' WORK.

Secret: *Fundraising work starts at the parental level, but both parents and the players (if appropriate) should work to raise needed funds. Players who do their part to help raise money tend to take more pride in the team.*

HAVE MONEY, WILL TRAVEL

It's no secret that it takes money, often lots of it, to run a baseball league, all-star team, or travel baseball team. These days, most academic, athletic, or extracurricular organizations are facing budget crises and shortfalls. Fewer resources are available to keep leagues and teams afloat. Whether your goal is to operate a team on a skeleton budget or to run a first-class operation with all the bells and whistles, chances are you will need the help of a booster club or fundraising to meet the budget for a league, all-star team, or travel team.

Effective booster clubs can be a way to supplement budgets to make ends meet or, in some instances, go beyond the league budget to make things special for your team or program. Booster clubs can be as simple as a group of parents who get together to organize a car wash to raise the money to pay a tournament entry fee, or they can be complex organizations with elected officers and large budgets.

Successful baseball programs and booster clubs realize that qualified people must coach the team if the players are going to reach their full potential. Effective baseball booster clubs, often called "dugout clubs," "base hit clubs," or "home run clubs," will set up committees that are ultimately overseen by the head coach. They will perform functions such as completing projects for the team, preparing the field for home games, organizing and operating the concession stand, and organizing the end-of-the-season banquet.

THE FOCUS

The focus of a booster club is to assist, not control, the baseball program. Booster clubs should operate on a plan set in motion by the head coach of the team. The head coach has vision, and he or she knows what it is going to take to succeed. The coach can present a wish list to the booster club, and the entire group can come up with strategies to provide what is needed for the team. Bobby Guthrie, Senior Administrator for Athletics in Wake County, North Carolina, states: "Coaches want parental involvement, but they have to put parameters on this involvement. Have parent meetings to let them know how they can help. This lets them know that boundaries are necessities."

It often helps to put long-range goals in place to give the booster club purpose and direction for years to come. It is important that the booster club does not try to take on too much financial obligation in one year and subsequently leave itself in a hole for future years. This can cause hard feelings for parents who are coming up into the program. They may feel they have been left to repair the damages of people who spent lots of money on their children but won't be there to help pay back that money.

If you are starting a booster club just for a travel baseball team, be sure to take the proper steps to set it up correctly and establish bylaws that clearly state the objectives of the club. Great things can happen when a group of people comes together with clear focus in purpose and sets aside personal agendas. Booster clubs can be an enormous resource for a baseball program and give the coaches the tools they need to be successful on the field.

PROCEDURES

The first order of business is to have a well-publicized team meeting and elect officers for the booster club. This should not be a popularity contest. Officers should be elected based upon personality qualities that will allow them to do the best job for their position. Proper business meeting protocol should be followed and minutes (records of what was said at the meetings and who said it) should be kept on file. These may be needed at a later time to set up booster accounts at the bank or application for tax-exempt status. Officers for a typical booster club should include president, vice-president, secretary, and a financial officer or treasurer.

The club president should have a business background, interact well with people, and not be easily misled by what other people think. The same goes for the vice-president. Though business backgrounds are not necessary, they are helpful for all officers.

The club secretary should possess good record-keeping skills. He or she should keep minutes of old business and provide copies of the old minutes to members at each meeting. He or she should also keep records of booster club memberships. Parents cannot vote at meetings unless they are up-to-date paying their team fees. It can be beneficial if the secretary has at least minimal experience with basic Web site management and can keep the team Web site current with booster club information. If not, someone else in the booster club can handle those duties. You may even want to create a special position just for that purpose.

The financial officer or treasurer ideally should have some banking experience and be good with numbers. He or she can help the club apply for tax-exempt status if that is a priority. The treasurer should provide current financial reports to all members at meetings so everyone can see how money is being spent. He or she can address any questions related to money. The treasurer can work with the coach to set up a yearly budget for the team based on needs and wants. This individual will keep the check-book up-to-date and keep a safe watch over booster club credit cards. All club accounts should be set up so more than one signature is required to withdraw money or write a check. It is imperative that coaches do not handle money in any way. This is the quickest way for a coach to get in trouble and possibly lose his or her job.

ESTABLISH COMMITTEES

Once the formalities of setting up the booster club are taken care of, the club should hold a separate meeting to establish subcommittees based on the individual talents of the club members. In order for a healthy, thriving booster club to exist, everyone should do his or her part and not leave all the work to just a few willing souls. If everyone makes a small sacrifice of time for their own specialized part of the club, a tremendous amount of work can be accomplished in a short period for the benefit of all.

Booster club committees can include, but are not limited to, ticket-takers, parking attendants, press box operators, field maintenance crews, concession stand operators, building project crews, fundraiser organizers, team Web site helpers, and end-of-the-season banquet organizers.

HANDLING MONEY

It has been paraphrased often that "Money is the root of all evil." With this in mind, you must have procedures and protocols in place to handle all booster club finances in a safe and accountable manner. Whatever the particular situation of each team, the one thing that must be consistent is the wise management of the team's money. I have heard of teams using all the money they raised for someone's personal vacation. If a reliable system isn't put into place, anything can happen. It is not a good feeling for bills to come due with no money in the account. This is especially true if the money has been mismanaged.

FUNDRAISING

Most baseball programs at all levels have to do some type of fundraising to complement their budget or completely support their club. Fundraising can

be a difficult challenge. Getting young players and their parents to participate can be frustrating. Coaches should expect and encourage all players to
participate equally in raising money for team needs. Depending upon the
age of the player, parents should give their child as much responsibility as
possible. As a result, players learn how to communicate with adults, raise
money for what's important to them, and do their part to help the team.

Young kids who are asked to sell products or services as a part of
their fundraiser should be accompanied by an adult at all times. However,
the child should be encouraged to do most of the talking and selling.
Consumers are impressed with children who can express why they need
to sell their products or services. On the contrary, parents who do all the
selling for their child, or worse, write a check for their child's financial
obligation to play on the team, are not using this valuable opportunity to
teach their child responsibility.

Players should wear their team uniform or hat and jersey while selling
items. They should target businesses, friends, and neighbors. Coaches
should set in place a reward system for players who bring in the most
sales. Players should be recognized in front of their peers. The rewards
should be substantial enough to motivate players to make larger sales
for future fundraisers.

Coaches should divide up their teams into small groups that can work
together. Each "mini-team" can be assigned a captain who keeps track of
sales and motivates his or her group. Another effective strategy, on the
last day of the fundraiser, is to group all the players together and do one
last mass sale. Partner the lowest sellers with the highest sellers and send
them out for one final attempt to raise funds. Give a separate reward to
the highest selling group (or pair) for that evening.

If you can establish a unique event or product that your community can
count on year after year, it can give your team an advantage in the fundraising battle. Everyone, not just athletic teams, is trying to raise money.
Businesses and individuals are growing tired of being asked for money
to help support teams and programs. As a general guideline, fundraisers
should provide a product or service that consumers can use. The team
should make at least a 50 percent profit from what it is selling. It is even
more advantageous when the fundraiser can provide a special need for the
local community, such as fruit around the Christmas holiday or a "turn back
the clock" home run derby. Some examples of fundraisers include:

- Fruit sales (oranges, apples, and so on).
- Hosting a wood bat baseball tournament.

- Holiday-related Christmas tree or pumpkin sales.
- Home run derbies, marathon games, or alumni games.
- Golf tournaments with silent auctions.
- Candy sales or magazine sales.
- Restaurant or business discount cards.
- Coffee mug sales (get one free fill-up at every home game).
- Raffles (vacations, TVs, computers).
- Pancake breakfasts, fish fries, or bake sales.
- Community poker tournaments or bingo events.
- Selling team "spirit wear" (clothing and other items with the team's logo or name).
- Selling priority seating for home games.
- Selling priority parking spaces for home games.

Once a fundraiser is completed, the booster club should mail thank-you cards to businesses and individuals who supported it. Coaches can write a letter to the local paper thanking the community for its support. Annually recognize your top financial donors with a letter suitable for framing and/or small souvenir.

BASEBALL FOR ALL

Participation in baseball can be very expensive. No child should ever be denied the opportunity to play baseball because of finances. Effective booster clubs set up a line item in the team budget for families who are not financially capable of meeting all the expenses associated with participation on the all-star or travel team. Coaches should keep a watchful eye for players who have trouble paying for basic team needs. No player wants to be embarrassed by going without, so he or she tends to make up excuses for not having basic equipment or money for food or other necessities. Coaches should tactfully bring this to the attention of the officers in the booster club, and some of the funds raised can go to the baseball needs of these families. However, these children and parents should make a good-faith effort to participate in all team fundraisers.

DANGERS TO AVOID IN BOOSTER CLUBS

As beneficial as booster clubs can be for youth baseball programs, they have the potential to cause a great deal of stress if they are not properly managed. Parents can become domineering at times. Motivated by hard feelings, jealousy, or spite, their goal may be to divide the team concept and "sink the ship." It is imperative that booster club leadership recognizes when this is happening and tactfully addresses the problem before it gets out of hand and does irreversible damage to the club.

Personal agendas, such as getting back at the coach or someone else in the club, can cause conflict as well. Not everyone is going to get along on a team or in a booster club. The objective is to remember that the clubs support our kids. If we put our own agendas aside and put the kids first, everyone wins.

Handling too many projects at one time is another danger that booster clubs must try to avoid. This can create significant team debt. Do not plan budgets based on money that you think the team is going to receive. That well may run dry, and you will be responsible for the bills that are incurred. Big ticket items, such as lights for the field, a new concession stand/press box, new playing surface, or indoor hitting facility can be very costly. Some booster clubs will take out loans to pay for these over a specific period of time. However, parents entering the booster club after the loan was taken can become reluctant to raise money for an item that makes up a big part of the yearly club budget.

FOR ONE AND FOR ALL

When booster clubs are run correctly, with the right focus, they can be very beneficial to a team or baseball program. Teams can accomplish goals that were once just a dream of the coach or players. Facilities can improve drastically. Equipment can be purchased to improve the skills of players. Uniforms and accessories can be bought to give the team a professional look and confidence. Ultimately, the greatest benefit of an organized and efficient booster club is that coaches can spend more time doing what they are hired to do—help the kids become the best baseball players they can be!

INDEX